e stories behind every song

RADIOHEAD
KARMA POLICE

James Doheny

CARLTON
BOOKS

This is a Carlton book

First published by in Great Britain by Carlton Books Limited 2002

Text copyright © James Doheny 2002
Design copyright © Carlton Books Limited 2002

ISBN 1 84222 621 5

Project editor: Lorna Russell
Picture research: Adrian Bentley
Art Director: Clare Baggaley
Art Editor: Adam Wright
Designer: Tanya Devonshire-Jones
Cover design: Alison Tutton
Production: Janette Davis

The publishers would like to thank the following sources for their kind permission to reproduce the pictures in this book:

Jay Blakesberg: 16-17, 36, 47, 50, 62, 138t; **Lebrecht Collection:** 94, 106; **London Features International:** 23, 60, 65, 86, 91, 113b, 136t; /ABACA: 1, 130, 131, 133br, 133t; /Awais Butt: 126; /Kristin Callahan: 12, 15, 74; /Katherine Davis: 3; /Mike Diver: 57; /David Fisher: 80; /Frank Forcino: 53; /Gie Knaeps: 20, 21, 49, 55, 76, 120, 134b; /Lawrence Lawry: 61; /Peter Lawson: 33, 138b; /Ilpo Musto: 114; /Tim Paton: 139tr; /Derek Ridgers: 4, 39; /Herb Snitzer: 136b; **Redferns:** /Glenn A Baker Archives: 8; /Mick Hutson: 113t, 133bl; /Max Jones Files: 119; /Michael Ochs Archives: 139tl; /David Redfern: 137tr; **Retna:** /Guy Aroch: 31; /David Atlas: 99; /Jay Blakesberg: 9; /Chris Denehy: 92; /Steve Double: 95; /Thomas Dubois: 118; /Robin Francois: 51, 69; /Dennis Kleiman: 40; /L.A. Media: 93, 105, 112; /Youri Lenquette: 6bl; /Brad Miller: 109; /Spiros Pollitis: 117; /Pat Pope: 28, 29; /Neal Preston: 88; /Ed Sirrs: 13; /Yael: 89; **Rex Features:** 6tl; /Rick Colls: 81, 122; /Huw Evans: 75; /Hayley Madden: 7; /Pasquale Modica: 132b, 132t; /Erik Pendzich: 42, 58, 101; /Pat Pope: 43, 46, 52, 67, 70, 73, 83, 85, 121, 134t; /Brian Rasic: 11, 41, 44, 135b, 135t, 137b; /Roger Sargent: 115; /SIPA: 125, 137tl; /Jeremy Sutton Hibbert: 97; /Stephen Sweet: 48; **Warp Records:** 90.

Every effort has been made to acknowledge correctly and contact the source and/or copyright holder of each picture, and Carlton Books Limited apologises for any unintentional errors or omissions which will be corrected in future editions of this book.

CONTENTS

"Remain orderly and modest in your life like a bourgeois so that you can be wild and creative in your work"

Arthur Rimbaud (This quote is known to be much beloved by Thom Yorke)

INTRODUCTION - ON A FRIDAY

Radiohead have proved to be an exceptional band in many ways, and this is as true of their history as of any other aspect of their career. One of the band's defining and most engaging features is the fierce loyalty that Thom Yorke (vocals and guitar), Jonny Greenwood (guitar and keyboards), Ed O'Brien (guitar and vocals), Colin Greenwood (bass) and Phil Selway (drums) have had for each other, and for the band, since its formation nearly eighteen years ago. Very much a family affair, not only have they maintained the same line-up from the outset, but it's difficult to see the band continuing were a member to leave. Eighteen years is a long time for any friendship, but particularly one forged so young and then subjected to the unique strains of rock superstardom.

Back in 1984, the five were school friends at the all-male Abingdon College in Oxfordshire. Though not one of the most famous public schools alongside Eton or Harrow, it's academically strong and has good facilities including a thriving music department which the band took full advantage of, learning a number of instruments. Most of its ex-pupils (with the noticeable exception of T. Yorke, Esq) seem to have enjoyed their time there.

Thom and Colin joined their first band, the school's punk outfit TNT, in 1982, when both were fourteen years old. Thom became the singer, "because no one else would". By 1984, the lads had decided that punk was dead after all. They left to start their own, as-yet-unnamed band, which would eventually become Radiohead. Ed O'Brien was the next member to join, followed by Phil Selway. Bringing up the rear was the baby of the group, Jonathan 'Jonny' Greenwood.

Taking the name On A Friday, a prosaic reference to the day the band rehearsed, the group's early music was a mixture of Joy Division, Magazine and The Smiths, plus Elvis Costello, U2, REM and Japan. Mostly written by Thom, it was a fairly typical who's-who of 1980s indie-dom.

When the time arrives to go off to college or university, most school bands gently fall apart as the members begin new lives in new places. Little survives beyond a collection of old photographs, happy memories and the occasional, often embarrassing, recording. On A Friday were very different, however, and if anything, when the inevitable dispersal began in 1986, it strengthened their resolve. The older members took to travelling back to Oxford to rehearse as often as they could. The following year they began to circulate their first demo tape, and played their first public live show at Oxford's Jericho Tavern, for which they were augmented by their occasional three-piece saxophone section. The band's enthusiasm for a sax section would fade away soon afterwards, only to resurface thirteen years later, in a vastly changed form, on the *Amnesiac* album.

Over the next few years, band logistics determine that they would mainly rehearse during school breaks. In the meantime, Thom honed his writing skills and struck up a fruitful creative partnership with Jonny Greenwood, who was still at school at the time. Perhaps the most musically talented of the band, Jonny would function as Thom's musical director, polishing off and putting in order Thom's sometimes roughly hewn compositions.

Important early influences, REM and The Pixies.

Two key influences, both musically and professionally, on all of On A Friday at this time were the American bands REM and The Pixies. Ed O'Brien explained to Mac Randall, in his book *Exit Music* (Omnibus Press 2000), "When we were sort of trying to get our shit together in 1989 and 1990, we were thinking about seriously trying to get a record deal once we'd finished college. REM and the Pixies were the two bands that we used to go down the pub and talk about after rehearsal. You know, 'They did it this way, and that's how we want to do it.' There was an ethic there that we admired, and it extended to much more than the music."

With Yorke graduating in 1991 (from Exeter University, where he studied English and Art) things got moving again in earnest. In April, the band booked into Dungeon Studios near Oxford to record a new demo of three songs – "What Is That You See", "Stop Whispering" and "Give It Up". Whilst the other two tracks were rather routine slabs of, respectively, REM and indie-dance, "Stop Whispering" would prove strong enough to go the distance and appear in a re-recorded form on *Pablo Honey*, the band's debut album.

The tape, simply entitled *On A Friday*, was distributed locally around the Oxford area. In addition to helping the band get gigs, it found its way to Chris Hufford, a local producer and studio owner. He was impressed enough by the tape to check out the band's next Jericho Tavern gig on August 8, 1991, and admits to being "completely blown away", particularly by Thom's super-intense on-stage performance.

Hufford offered On A Friday a cut-price deal to record their next demo in Courtyard Studios, which the band were only too happy to take up. Recorded in October, the result was christened *Manic Hedgehog* after the name of the independent record store in Oxford where it was sold. The tape features five tracks: "I Can't", "Thinking About You", "You", "Nothing Touches Me" and "Phillipa Chicken", and it's a sign of their growing maturity that the first three of these songs would find their way onto the band's first album *Pablo Honey*. The two tracks that eventually fell by the wayside were both former stage favourites, being a catchy ditty relating the imprisonment of a talented painter for child molestation and a quirky country-tinged confection respectively. All concerned were so pleased with both the results and personal chemistry that Hufford and Edge joined the Radiohead family as the band's managers, a position they hold to this day. All that remained before all the pieces were in position was the small matter of a recording contract.

Every successful artist relies on a bit of good luck, and Radiohead had received a major dollop earlier that summer in the form of a chance encounter between Colin Greenwood, then working in the local branch of Our Price, and EMI sales representative, and soon to be A&R man, Keith Wozencroft (the A&R department of a record company is responsible for signing and developing its artists). Wozencroft was actually on a farewell tour of his clients at the time, and while he was in the shop Colin had the opportunity to give him one of the band's April demos. A typical scene, but Wozencroft was impressed enough with the tape, and particularly the demo of "Stop Whispering", to come to see them live at an open-air gig in Oxford Park. He recalled to Mac Randall, "There was nobody there in this little tent, apart from a couple of their girlfriends. But they played really well."

Wozencroft reported back to EMI and in November brought his boss, Nick Gatfield, and the rest of the A&R team down to see the band. By then the band's management had carpeted the industry with copies of *Manic Hedgehog* and Wozencroft's interest had triggered a huge industry buzz. The gig was crawling with A&R men from different record companies, and in the weeks that followed the band were bombarded with contract offers – as is so often with the music business, either everything happens or nothing happens at all. The band nevertheless plumped for Wozencroft and EMI/Parlophone, and signed their recording contract at EMI's London head office on December 21, 1991. No longer a mere band, they were now recording artists.

PABLO HONEY
1993

Daniel Goleman's landmark book on psychology, *Emotional Intelligence*, contains this interesting passage: "Perhaps the most disturbing single piece of data in this book comes from a massive survey of parents and teachers and shows a worldwide trend for the present generation of children to be more troubled emotionally than the last: more lonely and depressed, more angry and unruly, more nervous and prone to worry, more impulsive and aggressive."

That list of adjectives is the psychological landscape of *Pablo Honey* in a nutshell. The quote also offers some clue as to the stellar success of "Creep" and to Radiohead eventually inheriting the position of the unofficial voice of a generation from the more upbeat and optimistic U2.

Having signed to EMI, it didn't take very long (around two months) for On A Friday to acquire a new name. Legend has it that Keith Wozencroft, unhappy with the band's name after a terrible first review in now-deceased UK weekly music magazine *Melody Maker*, wrote down the names of five songs on a piece of paper and "invited" the band to choose one. The favoured choice was Talking Head's "Radio Head" from the 1986 *True Stories* album. While the song itself is undistinguished, the choice of Talking Heads is indicative of a felt kinship and sense of purpose with the arty, intelligent, musically literate and subversive New Yorkers. The fact that Talking Heads had the world's twitchiest and most nervous front man probably didn't go unnoticed, either.

With EMI anxious to recoup some money on its investment, the band's first mission was to go back into Courtyard Studios to record the *Drill* EP with Chris Hufford at the helm. *Drill* featured two new songs, "Prove Yourself" and "Stupid Car", as well as the recordings of "You" and "Thinking About You" from the *Manic Hedgehog* tape. All but "Stupid Car" would find their way onto *Pablo Honey* after being re-recorded. Frankly, *Drill* is not the band's finest piece of work, with mixes, performance and some arrangements not really up to the mark. Not surprisingly in retrospect, it only managed a dismal number 101 in the UK singles chart.

In the UK of 1991-92, rock – particularly pre-Nirvana US rock – was being administered the last rites. Critical interest was focussed on dance music and electronica with bands like the Stone Roses and Happy Mondays striving to amalgamate the two. U2 were also taking these currents on board, recasting their sound for *Achtung Baby* (1991) and its offspring *Zooropa* (1993). Radiohead had some kinship with the UK's jangly guitar-driven "shoegazing" scene of Thames Valley bands such as Slowdive and Ride, but they wore their US influences too openly to fit in properly. Worse still, these were not even cool, avant-garde US influences (Beefheart, Sonic Youth) but rather the common-or-garden and (reasonably) wholesome staples of everyday college America – REM, The Pixies and U2 (honorary Americans, in this instance). Right from the off, Radiohead were clearly going to have a hard time with the UK critics.

Given all this, and the poor performance of *Drill*, the decision to put the band to work with US production team Paul Q. Kolderie and Sean Slade was undoubtedly wise. Band and producers set to work on the next single, "Creep", at Chipping Norton Studios near Oxford. The remainder of the album (bar two tracks) was recorded at the same studio in three short weeks, and after mixing back at Sean and Paul's Boston HQ "Fort Apache", would be released in February the following year.

It's become fashionable to knock *Pablo Honey*, not least as the band themselves have been rather dismissive of it. Ed O'Brien has described it as "a collection of our greatest hits as an unsigned band". It's true that it doesn't hint at the giant leaps that were to follow, but on its own merits it's a solid, varied and enjoyable debut with much to be admired. And, of course, it laid the foundations for everything that was to come.

The album's original review in *Melody Maker* summed up *Pablo Honey* rather neatly – "promisingly imperfect".

01 YOU

Threading its way from On A Friday's *Manic Hedgehog* cassette through the *Drill* EP, "You" found its way to *Pablo Honey* in a pretty much constant form. The simple reason for this was that it works so well. Say what you like about some of the other tracks on the album, "You" is a great piece that wouldn't be out of place on *The Bends*.

Overwrought and swooning in both lyrics and music, the track is about an infatuation so intense that it's on the point of being dangerous: "You are the sun and moon and stars are you and I could never run away from you." Alternately submissive and aggressively asserting his right to self-denial, there's a tremendous synergy between the lyrics and music as the singer's masochistic emotions run riot. A series of jarring contrasts in all musical departments underscores the bi-polar lyric as the song hurtles out of control to emotional meltdown: "You me and everything, caught in the fire. I can see me drowning, caught in the fire."

Thom's vocal is terrific, and he communicates at least as much with the timbre of his voice as with the lyric. "Frighteningly intense" is no overstatement, and it's easy to see what so impressed Keith Wozencroft about his performance. At no time do you doubt the sincerity of what he's singing: quite the reverse, in fact.

One of the most immediately striking facets of the track is the sheer visceral impact of the band's guitars. After Jonny's woozy, chiming intro, a fiery layer cake of guitars crashes in, the sonic equivalent of a punch to the stomach. As the first track on the band's first album, you can be sure that both producers and band wanted to start proceedings off with a suitable sonic bang. No worries there. Part of this intense effect is due to the blistering overdubs, but equally important is the churning effect of the song's irregular metre and ambiguous harmony.

Thom has said, "There was a need to put more and more guitar tracks on *Pablo Honey* – we'd have four rhythm guitar tracks, and everyone had to play a part." According to Ed O'Brien, "Sean Slade would say, 'I want fucking eight walls of guitars here, eight overdubs,' and we were like, 'Yeah, let's do it, that's great.'"

The idea of over-dubbing multiple layers of guitars has been around as long as multi-tracks, but the early 90s saw the perfecting of this kind of monolithic sound. In terms of the sort of impact the band summon here, people very often refer to Radiohead's "three-guitar sound" as if the number alone was a guarantor of effect. As elsewhere in life, it's not so much size as what you do with it that counts.

The key is Yorke's quote, "everyone had to play a part". On first hearing, "You" doesn't seem to have much in the way of independent lines, but if you listen closely you'll hear subtle differences: multiple versions of the same chord interlocking, different ways of playing the same chords, all manner of different guitar sounds. Given that the whole album was recorded in three weeks, this complicated arrangement must have been in place in advance. It may not have been spontaneous – but it was combustive.

That's not to imply that Radiohead's producers were resting on their laurels: far from it. You can hear the intricate ways the various instruments and effects are panned across the stereo spectrum, and how much work has been done to coax movement into that huge guitar noise.

A significant part of the song's swooning effect is down to the shifting number of beats per bar. Most of the song is in four-bar patterns of 6,6,6 and 5 beats respectively. Coupled with the swooping guitar pattern of the intro, this produces a lolloping, churning effect not unrelated to the state of our hero's insides. When the band drop into a more regular metre for the guitar breaks, the sudden release of tension gives the song a tremendous forward surge, which the band naturally do their best to exploit with propulsive heavy metal-style speed picking.

Another band fingerprint already in evidence is their delight in using unexpected chords and chord shifts, particularly between major and minor versions of the same chord. We can hear this in both the unusual main chord sequence (which is what keeps it refreshed), and in the killer chord substitution at the end of the verses.

Below: Nirvana

Jonny Greenwood cites jazz as an important influence on his writing, and these are all common jazz manoeuvres. What's unusual is for them to be used so convincingly in a guitar-driven rock band. It not only shows off Radiohead's musical skill, but also demonstrates their determination to go beyond established norms at this very early stage by wringing as much interest, excitement and freshness out of their music as possible.

02 CREEP

After the metrical trickery of "You", "Creep" seems a much more conventional affair on first hearing, and yet it was this track that was to propel Radiohead seemingly overnight to international stardom.

Things are never quite that straightforward in real life, of course, and when "Creep" was first released as a single in

"I don't think we can explain what the Americans like about us....."

the UK (on September 21, 1992) it bombed unceremoniously. Luckily, it was taken up on import by enthusiastic DJs in several countries, and gradually built momentum to become a huge hit. The US in particular loved "Creep", and the track became adopted as a Generation X anthem of affirmatory self-loathing and alienation second only to Nirvana's "Smells Like Teen Spirit": "I'm a creep, I'm a weirdo, what the hell am I doing here, I don't belong here."

While understandably delighted, the band themselves were somewhat bemused at the track's sudden success. Jonny Greenwood said at the time, "I don't think we can explain what the Americans like about us, but they do like classic English angst pop, and they seem to find us very English." It's worth noting, however, that Jonny doesn't actually describe the band as "angst pop" himself.

Though "Smells Like Teen Spirit" and "Creep" both carry a similar emotional charge by way of compelling writing and performance, and share an assured sense of dramatic structure and timing, they are in other ways entirely different. "Teen Spirit" is an electrifyingly intense and at times unintelligible tone poem, whereas "Creep" is an acutely observed and deftly executed monodrama of considerable subtlety. Obviously, this is not to say that one piece is better, worse or more "authentic" than the other.

The "storytelling" aspect of Radiohead's songs is an important and perhaps inevitable one, given that three members of the band – including Thom Yorke – majored in English at college. The story of "Creep" revolves round the ecstatic idolisation of an angelic female beloved, and the contrastingly wretched self-flagellation of the idolater. It's a powerful archetype (Dante and Beatrice, Lennon and "Girl", Woody Allen and any number of women) and one with which anyone who's ever been a teenage boy can readily identify. This puts at least half of the record buying public on Thom Yorke's side for a start.

"Creep" was actually quite an old song by the time of its release. Thom Yorke had written an early version whilst still at university in the late 1980s. His inspiration arose, he has revealed, from, "a rocky relationship I was having at the time". Now, you don't necessarily need a good education to feel painfully exposed and vulnerable when dealing with the opposite sex, but in Thom Yorke's case it certainly helped.

"Girls didn't figure in our lives for a long time," he's explained. "They were freaks of nature you saw every now and again, and wondered how they worked. I feel tremendous guilt for any sexual feelings I have, so I end up spending my entire life feeling sorry for fancying somebody. Even in school I thought girls were so wonderful that I was scared to death of them."

The usual adolescent feelings of shyness and painful self-consciousness were undoubtedly exacerbated in Thom's case by the problem he has with his left eye.

Fixed shut and paralysed at birth, it was later partially rectified with the aid of muscle grafts, but its eyelid still droops slightly. To us it may seem a minor blemish, but as an adolescent there's no doubt he would have been constantly and acutely aware of it. His classmates, who nicknamed him Salamander, made his problem a constant mocking/discussion topic.

Yorke's self-consciousness is desperately evident in his attempts to conceal his lazy eye in the band's early photos and in the booklet that accompanies *Pablo Honey*. Dark glasses or stilted head-turning are the order of the day. To what degree Thom was emotionally scarred or damaged by all this we can only speculate, but I think its fair to say that when he sings, "I'm a creep, I'm a weirdo," he's expressing many bitterly painful resentments. The whole experience may well have made him a better writer, heightening and honing his self-awareness, but it's a high, high price to pay.

"Creep" has a fairly conventional structure – verse, bridge, chorus, verse, bridge, chorus, mid section climax, verse, bridge, chorus – solidly underpinned by a constantly repeating eight-bar harmonic pattern and its associated bass line. This provides a steady platform on which the drama of the song is played out by its other constituent elements: lyrics, melody, intonation, performance, dynamics and orchestration, etc.

The very first words of the song are set to a melody that fits the chord awkwardly, the aural equivalent of Thom shuffling nervily in his shoes. The song gets scarier and more intensely unhinged as it progresses (as does "You"). The dramatic focus constantly shifts backwards and forwards in a series of tight, claustrophobic close-ups, from girl to narrator and back again, cutting across the usual boundaries of verse and chorus:

Verse 1: "When you were here before…"
Bridge 1: "I wish I was special…"
Chorus 1: "I'm a creep…"
get swapped around for:
Verse 2: "I don't care if it hurts…"
Bridge 2: "You're so fucking special…"
Chorus 2: "I'm a creep…"
As the focus stays trained on the girl as the song ends, we realise with a jolt that what had seemed a harmless if disturbing daydream is actually happening in real time. This change in perspective is given even more potency by the quicksilver shifts in Thom Yorke's voice. Flexible, enervated and emotive, his singing adds a further dimension to the drama, sometimes underlining the

narrative, at others contradicting or unexpectedly tinting it. It summons diffident humour: "You look like an angel, your skin makes me cry", as well as urgent intensity:"'What the hell am I doing here? I don't belong here".

The melody also has some interesting wrinkles, most particularly the lead in to the chorus "I wish I was special, you're so fucking special". As the words repeat, the melody and harmony shift mode, darkening from C major to C minor, making a deliberate mockery of the word "special" in the process. This combination of downwardly twisted melody and compressed harmony is a hugely potent one.

In deliberate contrast to all of this, the rest of the band generally keep things simple with gentle verses, loud choruses and a louder climax eventually falling back to a fragile reprise. In a piece without grand harmonic signposts, this is not only dynamically interesting but a navigational necessity. Within this broad framework, we can hear the same keen dramatic planning at work, and as the searing curtain of guitars that roars into life at the chorus overwhelms the tremulous arpeggios that accompany the song's verses, we can feel the flames of anguish barbecuing Thom Yorke.

"Creep" is a tremendous track with a depth and subtlety of composition and performance that are truly remarkable. That's why it stood out so vividly amongst the many (many!) other downbeat songs floating around in the early 1990s, but also why the "English angst pop" tag that it acquired just doesn't feel right. The Smiths are "angst pop" but "Creep" is something else, darker and more bruised.

As a platform on which to write music, the device of repeating a chord sequence over and over again can be found everywhere from the blues to the baroque passacaglia. In fact, "Creep" has a great deal in common with the blues – subject matter, performance style, ambiguous major/minor "blue" notes and infections (which are developed to form a pivotal part of "Creep"s melodic and harmonic language) – but at the same time it is a long way away from the classic blues of Robert Johnson. In a number of arcane ways, "Creep" also resembles a passacaglia – the chord pattern itself with those major/minor chord shifts, overlapping of lyrical and musical phrases to dramatic effect, etc. So, perhaps "Creep" is best described as a kind of dramatically self-conscious (in both senses) hybrid blues, the kind of late 20th Century English blues that Jimmy Page or Eric Clapton might have written if they'd been born a quarter of a century later than they were.

Amazingly, the version of "Creep" on *Pablo Honey* is practically a live recording, with everything apart from the piano and some snatches of vocal captured in one take. Giving us a snapshot of their concert sound at the time, it reflects well on the young band's professionalism and the level to which they were rehearsed. "Creep" delivered instant fame to Radiohead, but there was to be a Faustian sting in the tail. To their mounting dismay, Yorke and Radiohead found themselves stereotyped as "the Creep guy" and "the Creep band" for the next few years. Ed O'Brien told Mac Randall, "there was a point where we seemed to be living out the same four-and-a-half minutes of our lives over and over again. It was incredibly stultifying." Eventually the band could no longer refer to the song by name but only as "that song". The pop music equivalent of "the Scottish play", it was eventually banished from the band's live set for several years.

The song eventually climbed to number 34 in the US singles chart, pulling *Pablo Honey* to number 32 in the albums chart and gold record status. On re-release in the UK (on September 6, 1993, almost twelve months later) "Creep" reached number 7 and *Pablo Honey* number 25. Not bad for a hitherto unknown indie band from Oxfordshire.

03 HOW DO YOU?

On of the punkiest song that Radiohead have ever recorded, "How Do You" is unsurprisingly the shortest song on *Pablo Honey*, clocking in at a mere 2'12" (and even then the last half minute is a one-chord jam). It's a short and sour blast of open-ended condemnation wherein Thom tries to spit out the somewhat nebulous lyrics in the best punk fashion he can muster. He obviously wants to do a Johnny Rotten, but he and the band sound far more like Pete Shelley and the Buzzcocks: miserably suburban, and a bit whiny.

As the song is a punk pastiche, the band try to use a fairly limited chordal vocabulary, but still they can't help doing something interesting with it. The verse (in A) is very standard, but the chorus unexpectedly begins on G and then, still less usually, drops precipitously through a circle of fourths (G-D-A), the effect being somewhat like standing in a lift and having the floor suddenly fall away from you. Similarly, as with "You", we can hear the band's guitars artfully arranged for maximum presence, nesting various vertical permutations of the riff within each other rather than just banging the same riff out in true punk style. It's very cunning, but I shudder to think what Sid Vicious would have made of it. Toward the song's end the band decide that they're already bored with punk and decide to become Krautrock instead. The ring-modulated piano and dry metronomic drum pattern at the song's end are very reminiscent of early 70s Can, as is the recorded speech that can be heard low in volume on the right hand channel.

And what is this speech? Well, *Pablo Honey*'s title originates in an underground tape by New York phone pranksters the Jerky Boys which was doing the rounds at the time of recording. One of the skits starts with a Jerky Boy ringing up someone named Pablo and, pretending to be his mother, opening the conversation "Pablo, honey..." It's a desperately weak joke, but Thom apparently thought the title was appropriate because the band were all "mother's boys". It's so difficult to hear (headphones only), that it's only of interest to truly obsessive fans.

04 STOP WHISPERING

Originally the second track off On A Friday's first demo cassette, "Stop Whispering" is the oldest, longest (5' 25") and most basic track on *Pablo Honey*. The essence of the track is its anthemic, U2-esque journey from quiet to loud, a literal expression of the phrase "Stop whispering: start shouting", perhaps. Musically very simple, it has the kind of two-chord relentlessness that works well live where, largely freed from technical concerns, the band are able to enjoy themselves and respond more spontaneously to the audience and atmosphere.

It's notoriously difficult to capture the energy of these "vibe songs" in the studio, and so it proves here. Even though the structure has been tightened and the performance is certainly more even than the On A Friday version, the track still feels too long and the tension occasionally sags. Still, many far more experienced bands are guilty of much worse indulgences when it comes to pruning their live favourites.

Lyrically, as might be expected from the title, 'Stop Whispering' is a call to action and free expression. The verses paint a picture of the whole world (wise men, mothers, even buildings) actively trying to repress Thom. Such lyrics as, "I don't want to hear your voice", and, "We spit on you some more", seem to deny his very right to exist. Yorke tries to raise his voice in the third verse: "Dear Sir, I have a complaint", but he can't bring himself to articulate his ire. So, verbally

stymied, his frustration and anger are expressed instead in the music, which flares up angrily, building and building to the climactic "shout" before subsiding.

Underpinned for much of its length by Phil Selway's propulsive but unchanging brushwork, and with the same two chords circling endlessly over the top, the weight of articulating the song falls on Thom's dramatically sensitive vocal (which owes a major debt to Bono) and the changing instrumental texture, adding and occasionally subtracting more and more guitar layers as the song builds.

Again, we must remember that this is one of Radiohead's very earliest songs, and in its writing we can hear a nervous young band clinging to simple things, wisely concentrating on getting their sound to gel rather than mastering tricky chord changes. Nevertheless, the guitar arrangement is particularly tasteful with a varied and considered palette of sounds. A rather grim, record company inspired remix of the song was released in the US in December 1993 as a putative follow-up single to "Creep". Not surprisingly, it sunk without trace.

05 THINKING ABOUT YOU

Thom Yorke once confessed to *Rolling Stone*, "I feel tremendous guilt for any sexual feelings I have, so I end up spending my entire life feeling sorry for fancying somebody. Even in school I thought girls were so wonderful that I was scared to death of them. I masturbate a lot. That's how I deal with it." Those raw feelings, given a quasi-dramatic context, are what "Thinking Of You" is all about.

Although exploring similar emotional territory (guilt, anger, self-reproach etc) to "Creep" and using a similar lyrical device in the mood swings between self-pity and anger, the dramatic scenario of 'Thinking About You' has a interesting twist that keeps it fresh. Taken literally, the unreachable female is an ex-girlfriend who has dumped the singer (and now onanist) on becoming famous. Thus, though the song is in essence a common-or-garden soliloquy to lost love, the vivid detail it's painted in makes it personal and believable.

One of the older songs on *Pablo Honey*, the track was obviously a long-standing favourite with the band, and had been already released as the opener of On A Friday's *Manic Hedgehog* cassette and the final track of the *Drill* EP, the band's first single. That said, both of these are in a radically different and far more aggressive "electric" arrangement.

The band obviously (and, as it turned out, rightly) weren't happy with this and persevered until they had the very different arrangement we hear on the album. Recast as an airy piece of unplugged skiffle, it has a directness that suits the bedroom-bound lyric very well. Surprisingly enough, the track was apparently Jonny and Colin's mum's favourite on the album, but rather disappointingly this had more to do with the gentle new arrangement than anything else. "She had no idea it was about wanking," Jonny confessed to *Select* in May, 1995.

Vocally, Thom comes across as a hybrid of Shane MacGowan and Bob Dylan, somehow managing to mumble and howl at the same time. The lyrics portray a man unable to come to terms with his loss, constantly flooded by conflicting waves of emotion, and the ever-changing quality of Thom's voice reflects this superbly. To further emphasise it, and add some additional light-headedness, key words of the vocal are very lightly flanged.

Musically, the song pulls off a similar feat to the vocal, being both upbeat and self-pitying at the same time, an effect caused by the melody's strained relationship to the positive, but bluesy, chords beneath it. In fact, the melody constantly sounds as if it would rather be somewhere else. The driving, double-tracked acoustic guitars propel things along nicely, and Jonny spins in two lovely touches with a gentle Chet Atkins-meets-The Edge guitar solo and a warm harmonium in the song's climactic section. This use of organ is a Greenwood fingerprint that is also found in "You" and "Paranoid Android".

Last but by no means least, the barely perceptible kick drum and brushwork under the guitar solo speak volumes about Phil Selway's taste and restraint. Ironically christened "Mad Dog" by the rest of the band, Ed O'Brien has said of Phil, "He's very cerebral, he's very thoughtful...and he's not one to go smashing TV sets through windows."

06 ANYONE CAN PLAY GUITAR

Radiohead are not really in the business of producing catchy pop tunes, but the chorus of this song is the closest they've ever come. The rest of the song is, needless to say, the expected mix of caustic irony, searing guitar playing and abstract sound sculpture, but despite this the chorus was enough to propel it to number 32 in the UK singles chart. The band's third single had given them their first bone fide UK hit (the "Creep" phenomenon was still picking up steam around the world at this point).

The song is both an affectionate tribute and a leery debunking of the life-transforming power of the electric guitar: a typically Radiohead ambiguity. That said, there's no doubt of the transforming effect the electric guitar had on Thom Yorke's life When he was eight, Thom's parents bought him a Spanish guitar in a bid to cheer him up and help boost his confidence (he was being teased at school about his eye, and getting into fights). The portents weren't auspicious, as his previous guitar had ended up being smashed against the wall for hurting the young Yorke's fingers. One day, however, he heard a friend's copy of Queen's *A Night At The Opera* and was set aflame.

"I wanted to be Brian May," he recalled to Mick St. Michael in the CD booklet *Radiohead* (London: Virgin Sound and Media 1997). "I went into a guitar lesson when I was eight and said, 'I want to be Brian May'. I'd never wanted to be anything else. Before that, it was Lego."

In the various sections of the song, Yorke uses the guitar as a foil for examining his complex relationship to the idea of rock stardom. The verses are, on the surface at least, ironic and critical: "Destiny protect me from the world. Grow my hair, I wannabe, wannabe, wannabe Jim Morrison." However, the bridges are unreservedly positive: "I don't see no confusion anymore." The chorus is somewhere between the two, triumphal but somewhat melancholic, as if being famous was the only way of gaining self-worth: "Anyone can play guitar, and they won't be a nothing anymore."

As with many a hit single, the writing of "Anyone Can Play Guitar" started from the chorus and worked outwards. "We just hammered away at it for ages, and got all these nice clever bits in it. I didn't like the title, but everyone said, 'No that's the best bit, keep it,' so we did," Thom has explained. This was a shrewd career move, as it turned out.

Musically, as lyrically, there's quite a disparity between this rollicking anthemic chorus (somewhere between Springsteen and an Irish rebel song) and the other parts of the song. On one hand this makes for a series of interesting contrasts in sympathy with the lyric, but on the other it does create some sense of unlike parts being bolted together for effect.

It goes without saying that a song of this title, played by a band boasting no less than three inventive guitarists, would feature a lexicon of different guitar sounds (professional pride alone guarantees it). But not too many bands would begin their next radio-friendly hit single with a seventeen-second blast of improvised guitar cacophony in which their lead guitarist plays his instrument with a paint brush. Radiohead, on the other hand, would definitely do that, as producer Paul Kolderie reminisced to Mac Randall: "We rounded everyone up in the studio – all five band members, Sean and I, the studio owner, the cook – and gave each person a guitar. Everyone got assigned their own track, and they could do whatever they wanted. The idea was to live up to the title: anyone can play guitar. So they did."

07 RIPCORD

Pretty soon after the recording sessions for *Pablo Honey* had got underway, producers Kolderie and Slade had realised that the band, and particularly Thom, sounded their best when they were least aware of their performance. "Letting them get unconscious was the key," Kolderie explained to Mac Randall. "They are a band of destiny, as long as you just get out of the way and let it happen."

"Ripcord" has a palpable sense of this artless enthusiasm, and consequently is perhaps the freshest track on *Pablo Honey*. It's the sound of a happy young band growing in self-confidence, and stretching their musical wings. It's been suggested that the sketchy lyrics refer to fears the band had about losing control of (or worse still, being compelled to change) their artistic direction, on signing up to a major record label. There may be something in this but, by the time of recording, the lyrics' primary function was to act as a source of raw material for Thom's phonetic gymnastics.

You can hear Thom playing with the various parts of favourite words, chewing them around and nibbling on them for the sheer fun and effect of it: "In-Eh-vi-ter-Bul", "No-Rrrlpcord, Na-na-na-nar-no-rilpCord." At the start of the second verse he starts experimenting with his vocal resonance and sounds worryingly like *Carry On* movie stalwart Kenneth Williams: "AerhruPlaiyne, do ah mean whadarh meen?" On a more serious level, it shows a concern for the raw sound of a musical object divorced from whatever conventional function it may possess: the idea that was later to underpin the whole landscape of dislocation and re-synthesis on *Kid A*.

The rest of the band enjoy themselves just as much, with each player straining to cram as many different sounds and styles as he can into just over three minutes. There's sometimes a thin line separating exuberance and chaos, but the band steer a steady and picturesque course. The guitars leap like spring salmon from the zings and broken-speaker crackle of the opening, all the way to the massed ranks of the Radiohead string-string corps at the end. This chunky chromatic climax is reminiscent of Pink Floyd's "Astronomie Donomie" and, increasingly, of Queen.

Phil Selway's drum part is particularly impressive, not only running a stylistic gamut from Stax to 80s Goth-pop, but doing it whilst holding down another of the band's propulsive metrical fantasies (4 bar verse phrases of 4,4,2 and 4 beats respectively). As with "You", this keeps the verse sounding sprightly before it freefalls into weightless regularity for the chorus. "Ripcord" is an exuberant, good-time song from the people who would later bring you such party classics as "Exit Music (For A Film)" and "In Limbo".

"Letting them get unconscious was the key..."

08 VEGETABLE

Although musically this song seems to follow on from "Ripcord" as a kind of pastoral coda, lyrically it couldn't be more different. A poignant, country-tinged ballad, it tells a desperately sad tale of relationship breakdown and domestic violence. It's the kind of ghastly true-life confession you hope to only ever encounter on the most exploitative daytime TV shows. Merely listening to it makes you feel slightly squalid and voyeuristic. We're never properly told the full reason for the singer's all-too apparent agitation ("I'm not a vegetable, I can't control myself") other than that he finds his partner's words asphyxiating. However, being in the dark makes the descriptions seem even more frightening.

The scenario is so grim and the music so pretty that there's only one possible influence here – The Smiths. Radiohead have always been diligent students, and the start of this song is amazingly similar to the gloomsmiths' eponymous debut, from the open-tuned jangle down to the unusually (for Radiohead) funereal snare drum. After that, the song progressively goes its own way. Thom Yorke is not Morrissey, and by the time the chorus arrives we're in Elvis Costello-land. Then Attractions morph into Pixies for the guitar break, and we're in the home straight.

It's clear here that the band's formative influences are not yet entirely sublimated into a distinct, individual and coherent voice. It's all a bit lumpy, but at this stage that's probably not a bad thing. Radiohead, like all of the best bands, have decided that it's better to ruthlessly use and absorb their influences than to remain forever undefined and insipid. As T.S. Eliot put it, "Immature poets borrow, mature poets steal". Yorke has cited Elvis Costello (another cool-nerd craftsman in the manner of David Bryne) as a major influence, and this is apparent in the emphatic way he pronounces the chorus.

"I spit on the hand that feeds me," is a particularly idiomatic line. Try singing it on your own whilst clicking your fingers to the beat, and you will hear how mobile the tune is, and how kinetic the relationship between words, melody and beat. All the anticipations (rhythmic and melodic) give the music terrific impetus: when Yorke cries a discontented "I'm not a vegetable", you know that he really means it.

As well as borrowing from others, Radiohead have already developed more than a few of their own tricks, and one of the best of them is the way they use unusual metre to compelling dramatic effect. Each line in the verses is set over three bars comprising 4, 2 and 4 beats. Combined with the melody, this gathers tension into – and up through – the second bar (breathing in) before releasing it at the beginning of the third (breathing out, with a sigh). Put this together with the lyrics, and the effect is remarkably powerful: 'I worked hard/TRIED/hard/I never wanted any/BROKEN/bones'.

Picking out the emphasised words as an acrostic gives you the very essence of the song; Thing, Tried, Domestic, Died, Broken, No (home), (as)Phyxi(iate), All (hate). Now that's what I call... focused writing.

09 PROVE YOURSELF

As the album enters its last quarter, inspiration wears just that bit too thin to be wholly satisfying. It's as if the band only have a limited number of compositional elements available, and have gone through the more interesting permutations. Things become just that bit more derivative and repetitious, and interest and energy correspondingly start to flag.

The opening is once again in a similar harmonic area to the previous two songs, and some variation is surely overdue. The riff and subject matter are drearier cousins of "Stop Whispering", while almost everything else is lifted pretty much directly from The Pixies. Still, at least Thom has never been shy about acknowledging his influences: "The Pixies fucking rule. They were the best band ever, ever," he has previously pronounced.

Lyrically, "Prove Yourself" is obviously about the young band's desire to express and validate themselves: "I want to breathe, I want to grow, I'd say I want it but I don't know how". However, some of the imagery is frankly silly and the interminable repetitions of "I'm better off dead" begin to grate very quickly.

Given all this, and the fact that there were much stronger songs available, (e.g. "You", "Thinking About You", "I Can't"), it seems somewhat perverse that this was the band's choice to open their first major label single release (in a different, even less inspired form). Maybe that's why it was called the *Drill* EP rather than just "Prove Yourself". Such a title would have been just too ambitious, and too much of a provocation for the UK music press to tell his fledgling band how far they were from doing so.

10 I CAN'T

Originally the first track on On A Friday's *Manic Hedgehog* cassette, this upbeat slice of period indie-pop is one of the two tracks on the album recorded and produced at Courtyard Studios by Chris Hufford, and then subsequently mixed by Sean and Paul back home in the USA.

Another one of the band's early splicing-tape specials (as opposed to their much later, rather more deliberate digital productions), the track starts and finishes like Scottish indie guitar stalwarts Teenage Fanclub (a one time favourite of Phil Selway's) with a moody U2 breakdown interpolated in between. Given all this bravura cut-and-pasting, it's worth recalling Thom's time as a (quite successful) dance DJ while at Exeter University. "That was an excuse to spend loads of money on records and be a cult figure. It was great for my ego..." he's reminisced. Though similar in subject matter to "Vegetable" (the negative impact that the inability to control anxiety has on a relationship), "I Can't" is, thankfully, more positive, with the singer asking for understanding, forgiveness and even pity instead of using his fists. There are some nice touches in the lyrics (The pedantic, Morrissey-like "It wasn't me, it was my strange and creeping doubt", and the stuttering, "So many words that I, that I can never find"), as well as a few clangers ("If you leave me now, I'll be gutted like I've never been before").

The melody, on the other hand, breezes along merrily as if totally oblivious to all this earnest, human concern. In a rather Baroque manner, it's far more engaged in coolly abstracting every possible permutation of three rising and falling notes. Radiohead have clearly invested serious effort into this exercise in the craft of songwriting. Thus the chorus presents us with an ambiguous, emotionally complex picture. The lyrics speak of failure ("Even though I might, I try, I can't") while the music is positively triumphant. The glue holding the piece together is Thom's wonderfully mobile vocal, weary but hopeful, humbled by weakness but trusting to success.

The guitar work in the song is also very inventive, further honing instrumental and production scenarios (e.g. the filter sweeps in the opening Miles Davis-style counterpoint) that would come to feature more and more prominently in the band's future musical thinking. It's fair to say that "I Can't" looks forward, presciently, to the static sound sculptures of Kid A.

11 LURGEE

A word of explanation about the title is needed first. As fearful as it was ill-defined, the "dreaded lurgee" was a fictitious disease dreamt up by the late Spike Milligan, the tortured creative genius behind the pioneering 1950s British comedy trio The Goons. A running joke, the lurgee could be conveniently blamed for just about any illness or discontent as required. Hence, perhaps, the song's lyric: "I feel better now you've gone. I got better, I got strong. I got something, Heaven knows. I got something, I don't know".

How is the lurgee defined in a Radiohead context? "There's a pervading sense of loneliness I've had since the day I was born," Thom Yorke told *Rolling Stone* in September 1995. "Maybe a lot of other people feel the same way, but I'm not about to run up and down the street asking everybody if they're as lonely as I am. I'd probably get locked up."

This lurgee is clearly the unshakeable, energy-sapping sickness of the soul that you acquire when you've been deeply depressed for a very long period. As the comedian Milligan always suffered from acute clinical depression, it's a rather

"… a pervading sense of loneliness I've had since the day I was born"

appropriate title. Sadly, the title is easily the song's most compelling feature. The first of the two songs on the album to be recorded and produced at Courtyard Studios by Chris Hufford, this is pretty weak stuff. By this point on the album we really are starting to feel the band have exhausted their current stash of ideas and are merely reworking them ad nauseam.

Yet again, the song starts in a manner very reminiscent of "Reel Around The Fountain"-era Smiths. Its gently hypnotic, pulsing style of arrangement has a very long pedigree, stretching back through Johnny Marr, Sonic Youth and Steve Reich to the twin wellsprings of African blues and Indian classical music. The vocal's low-to-high melodic curve is developed in the jabbing guitar solo, which treks off on its own to explore various harmonic tensions and tints.

Overall, 'Lurgee' is pretty but insubstantial stuff which, ultimately, achieves little other than (hopefully) turning a few fans onto the comic genius of The Goons.

12 BLOW OUT

By now, as is often the way with bands' debut albums, Radiohead's early ideas are well and truly played out. They're clearly scrabbling around, but 'Blow Out' is no disgrace. A remixed version would later turn up on the UK single reissue of "Creep". Jonny and Thom have never been shy about acknowledging their love for jazz, but "Blow Out" is far-and-away the most overtly jazz-influenced track that Radiohead have ever released.

In overall shape, the song divides into two halves, with a stylistic shift from the Latin-tinged, jazzy opening to a much more indie-rock Pixies/Pumpkins finale. A nice cohesive touch is the way that the gently intermittent guitar of the opening returns as the furious feedback-laden behemoth of the finale. As in "Lurgee" the song slowly ascends its Live at Pompeii-ish way up the harmonic spectrum before finally squealing off into the outer darkness. Once again there's a plethora of different guitar sounds on show, but nothing that couldn't easily be reproduced live.

Lyrically, "Blow Out"'has the familiar Radiohead emotional landscape of disaffection, and depression: "In my mind and nailed into my heels, all the time, killing what I feel, I am fused just in case I blow out. I am glued just in case I crack out. And everything I touch turns to stone." While this certainly shows consistency, any interest in this particular corner of Thom Yorke's psyche might by now be wearing a bit thin, and after 42 minutes and 10 seconds you can't help feeling like sitting Yorke down with a cup of tea and telling him to lighten up! "Blow Out" isn't a perfect album closer, but it's still reasonably diverting. The closing extended instrumental section at the end is excellent, but – because it follows two other songs that use the same gambit – it simply seems just too familiar to be totally satisfying.

THE BENDS
1995

The phenomenal international success of "Creep" in 1993 meant that Radiohead appeared to have suddenly woken up globally renowned. *Pablo Honey* was selling by the truckload and, amongst other territories, had made a huge impact in the US. Predictably fêted as the heirs to REM, U2 and Nirvana, Radiohead were thrown roughly into a seemingly endless cycle of touring and promotion. They progressively raised their profile and sold out larger and larger venues, but as they clocked up the miles they were starting to discover that fame costs.

Naturally, as the band's career mushroomed, the pressure to deliver an impressive sophomore album mounted. Wisely feeling the need to put some physical and mental distance between things, Radiohead returned home from the US, where they were increasingly lauded, to the UK, where they most definitely were not.

It may be a truism that a prophet is never appreciated in his own land, but the UK rock press reserves a special odium for musicians who make it big in the US without having the courtesy to first do so at home. Radiohead soon found themselves either ignored, dismissed as purveyors of "major-label pop fodder" or, worse still, grouped with pariahs such as Bush, Wang Chung and The Fixx. They'd become outsiders on their own music scene.

In order to help them produce that "difficult" second album, which proves the graveyard of many a promising career, Radiohead enlisted

01   Planet Telex
02   The Bends
03   High And Dry
04   Fake Plastic Trees
05   Bones
06   (Nice Dream)
07   Just
08   My Iron Lung
09   Bullet Proof...I Wish I Was
10   Black Star
11   Sulk
12   Street Spirit (Fade Out)

the help of veteran English producer John Leckie. Typically, this was not because of his more famous work on The Stone Roses' first album but for his production of Magazine's 1978 debut *Real Life*, a Radiohead favourite. Leckie was also known to have a calm, "hands-off" production style that the band thought might be ideal. They were proved more right than they could possibly have suspected.

Sessions began in early 1994 at RAK studios in north London. Though something of a departure for the hitherto deliberately Oxfordshire-based band, this was still far removed from the febrile excesses available in the US. The resident engineer at RAK, a Leckie prodigy named Nigel Godrich, was to become a very important member of the Radiohead team. The group went into the studio knowing they had to "do something that was brilliant."

Apparently at EMI's suggestion, a large part of this first two months of recording was spent chasing a hit single to follow up "Creep" and herald the new album. This, Jonny later told Mick St Michael, was, "a very bad idea, because it set the album on a really wrong track." Worse, nobody seemed to agree on what the "hit single" should be.

The clock ticked and pressure mounted. Every few days, emissaries were sent by the record company to check on progress, but week after week after week went by with nothing tangible to show for it. "I couldn't have been more freaked out," Yorke told now-defunct UK music monthly magazine *Select*. "It has got to be the hardest thing I've ever, ever done...a total fucking meltdown for two fucking months."

The band were firmly stuck in the doldrums... and also suffering an advanced case of studio-phobia. Strange as it might seem in the light of *Pablo Honey*'s exuberant guitar effects, the band had "never really looked at the studio as an extension of what we were doing, more as an obstacle to get around."

Eventually, Radiohead decided to refocus on what they actually wanted to do, as opposed to any external (or internal) pressures and expectations. As Jonny recalled to Mac Randall, "The best part about working with John Leckie was that he didn't dictate anything to us. He allowed us to figure out what we wanted to do ourselves."

After a prearranged three-month tour of Europe and the Far East, a two-week recording session was convened at the rural splendour of Richard Branson's The Manor studios. There, the band explained in

The Mojo Collection (Mojo Books), "we got more done in those two weeks than we had in two months."

The band were intent on taming the studio and its technology and getting it to work for, rather than against, them. "John Leckie was very good at getting us to see the studio in a different way and taking the mystique out of it, almost making it like a musical instrument that you're learning to play," Jonny told *The Mojo Collection*. "Using the technology in front of you to actually write something completely opened my head to how we should be doing things. There was no longer any sense of intimidation - almost the exact opposite."

Newly inspired and empowered, Radiohead underwent a change of seemingly Damascene proportions. Suddenly in possession of a new maturity of musical vision, songwriting and musicianship, they finished *The Bends* with breathtaking speed.

However, one trauma remained before the release of *The Bends*. After finishing up the recordings in Abbey Road's legendary Studio 2 ("The Beatles Room") the Leckie-mixed "My Iron Lung", was released as a single on September 26, 1994. As the first product of all this hard work, expectations were naturally very high. It flopped badly, peaking at number 24 in the UK chart and selling less than 20,000 copies in the US.

Nervousness once more descended and EMI, anxious to secure a more "American sound" – as if that alone would guarantee a repeat of the success of "Creep" – took the master tapes of *The Bends* away from Leckie. *Pablo Honey* producers Slade and Kolderie were brought back in to do the final mixes of all but three tracks.

Leckie's commented to Mac Randall wryly: "The thing with *The Bends* is, if you put the multi-track tape on and just put the faders up, it would sound hardly any different from the finished record, because that's the way it was recorded, with very natural and organic sounds."

Kolderie seemed to concur: "John Leckie did an amazing production job on The Bends. There's not much we could have done if the tracks were lousy, but the tracks were great, and that's a tribute to him.'
The Bends was finally released in March 1995, to the

delight of most critics. In the UK music media, Radiohead were speedily upgraded from "major label pop-fodder" to "the defining band of the era".

However, despite this critical support the lack of a hit single meant the album lagged in the US,reaching only number 88 in the album chart, and that on the back of extensive touring. In the UK, however, *The Bends* stormed to number 6. By Christmas 1995, it had topped "Album Of The Year" magazine polls around the world: *People*, *Musician*, *Billboard* and the UK's *Melody Maker* and *NME*. Radiohead were even asked by their teenage heroes, REM, to open on their Monster tour. It seemed *The Bends* was their favourite album of the year, too.

Ever since then *The Bends*' reputation has continued to grow. In venerable UK music monthly magazine *Q*'s fifteenth anniversary poll (September 2001) *The Bends* was voted the fourth best album of the magazine's existence, behind Nirvana's *Nevermind* (3), Primal Scream's *Screamadelica* (2) and, er, *OK* somethingorother.... (1).

The essential sound of *The Bends* is that of a rock band. They're informed, influenced and facilitated by the techniques and methods of the recording studio, sure, but they're still very much a rock band. It's this tension that makes it a truly great album. Yet despite being a quantum leap from *Pablo Honey*, *The Bends* is still very much about the unique sound that voices, strings, drums and amps make when played live together in a single room.

The Bends, in this author's opinion, is a superior album to U2's *Achtung Baby*, to which it is often compared. Radiohead's reaction to, and synergy with, the possibilities and technologies of the studio simply permeated their music to a far greater extent. It is utilized at a compositional level rather than simply being a series of treatments applied, however brilliantly, to the surface. After their early '80s encounter with echo, U2's music was never fundamentally changed again by their experiences with studio technology, whereas Radiohead underwent a profound, flexible and honest artistic response.

Often cited as the *Revolver* to *OK Computer*'s *Sergeant Pepper*, *The Bends* seemed, for the moment at least, the apotheosis of what a rock group could do in the technological age while still remaining a rock group rather than breaking down roles and simply becoming a compositional collective. Mind you, that was true of *Revolver* too...

01 PLANET TELEX

Throughout *The Bends* there are basically three interrelating themes shaping and permeating everything from songs to album cover:

1) Alienation

Not just from one's surroundings, friends and loved ones but from many aspects of one's own self – personality, desires, opinions, dreams, even one's own body.

2) Transformation

From one place, environment or form to another.

3) Mechanization

The impact of machines on both of the above, and the feelings this produces.

One reason for the consistent use of medical imagery in both the lyrics ("My Iron Lung", "The Bends", "Bones") and on the album sleeve is that it's a particularly personal and powerful way of referring to all three defining themes at once. It's doubtful, nonetheless, that Radiohead clinically calculated this way of working. However, had they done so, it's unlikely to have been remotely so effective. *The Bends*, like all great albums, is simply an organic product of their feelings, interests, knowledge and experiences at the time. Indeed, things don't get much more organic than the making of "Planet Telex" and yet in it we see the band's most extreme (and almost literally unconscious) reaction so far to the recording studio and its technology.

The version of its origin that has passed down into Radiohead lore, and apparently confirmed by John Leckie (to Mac Randall) is as follows. One evening during the first frustrating sessions at RAK, the studio's chef decided he was going to have the night off, with the result that instead of eating in the studio as usual, all concerned decided to go out to a local restaurant. On the way home afterwards, suitably fuelled with food and alcohol, it was decided to "get something together in the studio". Thus inspired, some samples from "Killer Cars" drum track were looped up, Thom banged out the opening chords as the piano was feverishly patched into multiple space echoes and Jonny clanged some Telecaster through his home made tremolo. Hey Presto! – "Planet Telex". A couple of hours – and rather more beers – was all it had taken to break their studio-block and capture the essence of this monumental track.

As to the small matter of the lead vocal... "It was four o'clock in the morning," Thom somehow recalled to *Vox* magazine, "and John Leckie said, 'We've got to do the vocal now.' Ed remembers it better than me, but apparently I sang it all with my head on the floor because I couldn't stand up. I was bent double, and I hadn't got a clue what I was singing."

The band originally wanted to name the track "Planet Xerox", but the

> "Apparently I sang it all with my head on the floor because I couldn't stand up..."

eponymous corporation denied permission. Mind you, given the opening words ("You can force it, but it will not come/You can taste it, but it will not form", plus the howling, anguished refrain ("Everything is broken"), you can hardly blame them.

Yet "Planet Xerox" would have been a terrifically insightful and appropriate title, as a primary reason for the juddering power of "Planet Telex" is the incredibly close relationships between its various musical parts. It's almost as if somebody had put some of the band's best previous music under the compositional microscope, photographed a couple of choice motifs, replicated these in a musical Xerox machine, and then arranged the pieces tightly together – stacking, turning and magnifying them in various ways.

As in the less-effective "Lurgee", keeping some musical pieces absolutely static while moving others against them creates a trancey, psychedelic feel. It's rather like the constantly oscillating, but ultimately stationary, hypnotic chromaticism of a snake charmer. In "Planet Telex" this happens at a fundamental, even genetic musical level. This crystalline intricacy of rhythmic organisation in "Planet Telex" is unusually subtle in the west, but routine in India. This differential was recognized by Led Zeppelin, who used practically the same set-up for their similarly majestic "Kashmir". The rhythm gives both songs the same epic rooted quality as they roll inexorably onward like the wheels of Hindu 'juggernauts'. They're travelling on the outside, stationary in the middle.

Turning our attention to the rest of the music, we've already seen in songs like "Creep" that the band love playing with the colours of chords (chromatic alterations) and also flying sustained, undulating lines over the top of songs ("Blow Out" being an example). "Planet Telex", though, splices the two elements together with a concentration of purpose not seen before.

Harmonically, the basis of the song is very simple: Take a single note. Walk it two notes down, and then reflect it back again. Do the same over three related chords – B and A for the verse, and E – and, basically, that's it for 4'19" minutes. Colin anchors things down nicely with a lolloping John Paul Jones-meets-Peter

Hook bass line, while the autonomous upper notes wheel and play like seagulls round a minaret. In a remarkably concise way, this three-note motif generates almost every other melodic move in the song.

What gives "Planet Telex" its peculiar, more desolate character is the way the band take the underlying "mechanical" processes of its composition (replication, transformation etc) and make them that bit more apparent. The resulting tension between the "natural" (Thom's anguished cries, the basically acoustic sounds of the piano and guitar) and the "constructed" or "artificial" (the constructivist techniques, the supra-natural technology and effects) is where much of the interest lies.

So is Man extending himself naturally through the "Machine", or is the "Machine" squeezing Man into its own shape? Does the truth lie somewhere in between, and if so what are the consequences? While we're making our decision, we're treated to some fabulously old school sci-fi atmospheres along the way, the windswept space echo feedback at the start being a cautionary case in point. Once a clearly human sound, it has been repeated and repeated until its essential character is no longer discernible: it's just a disembodied machine noise floating in space, its defining humanity lost on the edge of an echo somewhere.

At the close of the song, just after Thom has given up imploring "Why Can't You Forget?" an elegiac Beatles-like guitar arpeggio enters. The returning space echo immediately menaces it, and we realize that this is where the sound had originally begun (a nice bit of symmetry). The contrast between the two is extremely disturbing, like seeing your loved ones' faces in burnt up photos.

In its ambition, ethos and use of sound, this opening song on *The Bends* very much anticipates what was to come on *OK Computer*. Wherever "Planet Telex" is, it's a long way from Pablo Honey.

02 THE BENDS

'The Bends' is the only Radiohead song which is also an album title, which gives an idea of its importance in their scheme of things. Its take on the corrosive consequences of fame is something that by now resonated only too strongly with the young band as they were swept wildly upwards in the wake of "Creep"'s success. In one way or another, it's a concern that permeates every other track on the album.

The jarringly evocative title refers of course to the crippling disorder suffered by divers who rise from the depths too quickly. Depending on the speed of ascent and the consequent bubbling of nitrogen in the bloodstream, it can cause agonising pain (causing sufferers to double over, hence the name), delirium and in the severest cases death, as blood vessels haemorrhage and explode from within.

It's a very extreme reference, but obviously that's how strongly the band felt about what was happening to them. As they told *Mojo* magazine, "Success is a weird thing. It really isolates you. We've always as a band kind of floated along in our own bubble, but when you're touring America and you're in this perpetual state of movement without really getting anywhere and everything's taken care of for you, it's so isolating. It's very lonely, but it's also very inspiring. There's this sense of being exposed to lots and lots of different crazy stuff, and being forced to consider it in isolation – and as a band we've always worked best in isolation." This latter sentence is as true of this song as it is of the album as a whole.

Despite its obvious topicality for the band the song is actually quite an old one, predating *Pablo Honey* and often played live previous to its recording. All this practice was obviously to good effect as the band apparently recorded the whole track at The Manor in a single take. The story is that Phil wanted to get things over quickly as he had a pressing real-estate appointment. Whatever the reason, the track positively crackles with seething, nervous energy. However cerebral the band might be, they can certainly rock out with considerable gusto.

The lyrics of the track are a reportage of despair, alienation and loneliness, most particularly as exacerbated by life on the road: "I'm just lying in a bar with my drip feed on, talking to my girlfriend and waiting for something to happen".

Radiohead were of course by no means the first musicians to suffer from this syndrome and there's a crushingly obvious parallel to be drawn with Pink Floyd's all-time public school favourite *The Wall*, which deals with exactly the same subject in a not dissimilar manner.

If the spirit of Roger Waters is abroad in the lyrics, then a Queenly ghost also hovers faintly over the music. The dry mobile guitar work in particular is an echo of *Sheer Heart Attack* and *News Of The World*.

The strongest parallel with the work of Freddie & Co, though, is definitely in the song's "jump-cut" multi-part structure and quicksilver changes of style. As in a mini-opera, the band are using the song's montage structure as a dramatic device, striving to give us a documentary, stream of consciousness sensation of what touring actually feels like. It captures the uniquely bewildering mix of crushing repetition and constant novelty, right down to the opening atmospherics recorded outside Thom's hotel window in Phoenix, Arizona.

03 HIGH AND DRY

If the first two tracks on *The Bends* came as a surprise, then "High And Dry" was a complete revelation.

Radiohead had released acoustic numbers before, but only as B-sides. There'd been nothing at all like this. A soaring, Crowded House-style arena-

singalong, however melancholic, was definitely not most people's idea of a Radiohead song. As *The Bends* progressed, however, it became clear that far from being an aberration, "High And Dry" was the first of a whole series of broadly acoustic tracks that was marking the beginning of what was to be an important new direction for the band.

As well as being the oldest recording on *The Bends*, "High And Dry" has a long and surprisingly tortured history that quite belies its more positive character. Its roots stretch right back to Thom Yorke's murky post-punk past. While a student at Exeter, Thom was moonlighting from On A Friday to play with college post-punk band Headless Chickens. "High And Dry" was just an item on their not overly extensive set list that, unusually for an anarchist punk combo, also included a cover of the Prince song "Raspberry Beret".

When played to his On A Friday band mates, however, Thom's demo of the song didn't engender a favourable reaction. It was based around a sampled Soul II Soul beat, and not only were dark comparisons to "Mull Of Kintyre" and "Maggie May" bandied around, but the band found themselves quite unable to get the groove together properly. As a result, "High And Dry" was quietly binned and featured on neither of On A Friday's cassettes. This is something of a pity as, in retrospect, it's obviously one of the best songs they had available.

The track didn't properly resurface until early 1993 when, somehow finding space in the middle of their heavy tour schedule, Radiohead booked into their managers' Courtyard Studios for the "Pop Is Dead" recording sessions which also produced the acoustic B-side "Banana Co.". With live soundman Jim Warren at the controls, they began recording the version of the track that would eventually surface on *The Bends*. Despite this, the band still weren't seduced by the track; "It sounded fucking dreadful", Thom confessed. Only when *The Bends* was recorded over a year later did "High And Dry" finally begin to make any real sense to Radiohead.

When released as the second single off the album (it's an established music biz convention that the second single is often a ballad), the song reached a creditable number 17 in the UK singles chart. The album itself was released two weeks later and reached a very impressive UK number 6 in 1995, eventually climbing to number 4 the following year – rather better than *Pablo Honey*'s number 25. The band had finally "arrived" in their home country.

04 FAKE PLASTIC TREES

"The simple songs", as they say, "are always the best", and so it is with "Fake Plastic Trees" and "The Bends". On one level the "simplest" song on the album, it is also the most affecting and profound – a combination one often finds in great music and which goes a long way to defining it.

Thom has described the song's origin as, "A very nice melody which I had absolutely no idea what to do with, and then...you go to sleep and you wake up and you find your head singing some words to it."

Threaded like beads along the plaintive unadorned melody, the song's vivid lyrics paint a detailed picture of contrasting images and concerns. Seamlessly moving from the darkly comic to the earnestly sincere and back again, the lyrics relate the story's disturbing and often surreal details in the comforting, repetitive style of a children's rhyme. It's a terrific contrast thrown into sharper relief by comparison with the music's gentle though ever-stronger lullaby. The quality of the lyric writing is exceptional too, and if Thom's powers of fantastic invention were working in overdrive, so was his ability to pin down emotion: "She lives with a broken man/A cracked polystyrene man who just crumbles and burns".

Thom would often quote "Fake Plastic Trees" as being the song in which he found his own lyrical voice, and it's hard to disagree with him.

When the time came to record the song, Thom put down his truly exceptional vocal and acoustic guitar performance in a single take, leaving his bandmates (and additional string players) with the unenviable and difficult task of having to write and perform everything else around him. The wonderful string part written by Jonny and Thom, and played by session cellist Caroline Lavelle and ex-Headless Chicken John Matthias on violin and viola, was multi-tracked the following day. The rest of the band followed on with their parts soon after.

When people discuss "Fake Plastic Trees" they usually refer to it as just a searing indictment of fakery and insincerity. While that's true on one level and a possible interpretation to draw from the lyrics alone, it ignores the powerful "feel-good" effect of the

music and so doesn't do proper justice to the song as a whole.

A plausible (if commercially questionable) subtitle for a book on Radiohead's music might be "Sad but Uplifting Modal Songs in Major Keys" and the band is at it again here. Though the music's melody and harmony are slightly unresolved, giving them a fragile and folksy quality, the song's slowly but remorselessly blossoming texture (particularly Jonny's ethereal filtered Hammond, the ecstatic strings and the thunderous climax) are very positive, telling us that "good spiritual things are happening" (Hammonds are a famously useful device for evoking the spiritual or epic).

This disparity is what gives the track, and a lot of the band's music, a Scott Walker-esque quality. The lyric may be telling us, "The sun ain't gonna shine anymore", but the music is saying that the sunset will last forever.

Putting all of this together gives us a more rounded picture of the song, roughly "inauthenticity vs positivity vs plaintiveness". It's that rare, white unicorn of the pop world, a genuine "anthem" (helpfully defined by the dictionary as a song of praise or gladness for antiphonal use – i.e. to be sung by both choir and congregation). Although "anthem" is undoubtedly the single most abused word in pop music writing, I think it definitely applies here.

In the final analysis I think that "Fake Plastic Trees" is an anthem of both acknowledgment and of reconciliation – a testament, as they put it in gospel circles. We catalogue and acknowledge our weakness and venal imperfection, but in reconciling ourselves to them we are also able to quietly celebrate our basic humanity.

Another less obvious, but not insignificant, contributor to the impact of the track is its position on the album and its relationship to the tracks that precede it. By the time we get this far into the album, we've already been on quite a varied musical journey, with the previous songs working structurally in a way rather akin to the movements of a mini-symphony ("Planet Telex" – atmospheric overture/ terse 1st movement, "The Bends" – playful scherzo, "High and Dry" – airy slow movement). There's already a momentum and an expectation for something weighty and finalizing even before the track starts, and luckily it doesn't disappoint. When the gorgeous string climax hits, it's closing an arc that began with the rising and falling opening chords of "Planet Telex".

"Fake Plastic Trees" was released as the 3rd UK single from the album on May 15, 1995, two months after the album itself. Though trailing in the album's wake, it still managed a creditable number 20 in the UK singles chart.

05 BONES

"Bones" is a relatively straightforward song that contrasts the before-and after-effects of severe depression and/or a nervous breakdown. "I used to fly like Peter Pan, touching children with my hand," Thom recalls, before admitting, "Now I can't climb the stairs, pieces missing everywhere, Prozac painkillers". Those critics of Radiohead's music as "miserable" could find ammunition here.

The hub of the song is Thom's strained chorus. Angular in the extreme, its notes start off widely spaced and then get even more spread-eagled. You can hear just how hard Thom has to work, darning the eight notes together in a Dylanesque fashion. As with Bob himself, it's always touch and go whether he'll make it at all, but it's a clever and very effective piece of writing.

Appropriately enough, the song was quite an effort to record, being a casualty

of the tortured RAK sessions. As Thom told *Vox* magazine, the band originally had the ending going on for about a minute and a half, "which was something that Jonny got from The Fall". Taking a break from the studio and playing the song live for a while proved restorative, and the final version was laid down at The Manor on the same day as "The Bends". There was a light at the end of the Prozac bottle after all (a definitively mid-'90s reference, that one).

Lyrically, we're both relapsing to "Lurgee" and exploring medical matters in a similar way to "The Bends" and "My Iron Lung". However, unlike these latter two songs but in the same way as much of *Pablo Honey*, "Bones" is a straight description rather than a metaphor for something else.

Another throwback, this time to "Vegetable", is the way that the entire song is grouped into bars of 6, 4 and 4 beats. The words are then draped across this metrical skeleton, emphasizing the first and – especially – the last key words of each line. When combined, in the chorus, with the tick-tock athleticism of Thom's vocal high jumps, the chiming effect is doubly strong: "GOT to feel it in your BONES.'"The skeletal "opening the back of the clock and seeing how the wheels turn round" precision of the process nicely mirrors the title. The guitar work, on the other hand, seems to be look ing backwards, sideways and forwards all at once. Just as a new "boogie" slant is brought to *Pablo Honey*'s indie rock party, the energetic, free-spirited tremolos look ahead to the ambient soundscapes of *OK Computer*. Finally, the way the static, pulsing guitar is used to counterpoint and echo Thom's ticking chorus touches on a line of development that leads all the way back from "Lurgee" through the oscillating "Planet Telex" to the mechanically precise sound sculptures of "Kid A".

All in all, then, "Bones" is a track perhaps more interesting for where it's been and where it's going than where it actually is.

06 [NICE DREAM]

The third acoustically driven number on *The Bends*, "Nice Dream" was one of the RAK session contenders for a potential single. Written back in 1992 and apparently based on a real dream of Thom's, the "nice dream" of the title is the primal urge to belong somewhere. On *Pablo Honey* this would undoubtedly have been explored in a straightforward, and most likely accusatory, first person shriek. Here, as with "Fake Plastic Trees", Thom chooses to explore the subject by way of a beautifully painted if surreal little story.

The matter-of-fact combination of fearless self-examination, dry humour and acid psychedelia set in a shifting sonic world of acoustic guitar, chamber strings/ Mellotron, Clapton-esque rock and filtered whale/tape noise effects definitely puts us in Beatles territory here. *Magical Mystery Tour* meets the "White" album, perhaps? That Thom Yorke was born in the year the "White" album was released adds to the sense of warmly remembered memories going horribly wrong.

The jazzy opening guitar chords have both the same progression and the same effortless cool as Brazilian composer Anthony Carlos Jobim's "One Note Samba", in which the held ringing upper note is extended to become the actual melody of the entire song. Radiohead aren't feeling quite that languorous, though, and as the band kick in, the guitar arpeggios throw the first piece of dissonant grit in the oyster.

Through the lovely, hymn-like verse, Thom tells us how happy he is: loved like a brother, protected and listened to. The chorus is more plaintive and static. With just a hint of chordal worry at the end to trouble things, all is basically well in Thom's dreamworld. As can so easily happen in Radiohead's music, however, things go very wrong very quickly and we're plunged into sinister weirdness that wouldn't be out of place in Neil Gaiman's *The Sandman*. Thom calls up his friend the good angel for help, but she's out socializing with her answerphone, and in any case the sea would electrocute everyone. Hmm. The strings provide a musical-hall "wavey" background to add to the queasiness and theatricality.

In addition to the "stream of consciousness" changes in the song's lyrical and musical elements, the ever-shifting relationships within the song are tremendously evocative of a dream-state. As such, the song's structure, with all its twists and additions, becomes a front-line storytelling device, a technique that will become increasingly prominent in the band's future music.

Thom initially seems to have been perfectly happy with the song as just the simple verse and chorus, and was none too impressed when Jonny and the band started making additions to it. He even confessed to hating part of the intro for a full two weeks before enthusiastically coming round to decide it was one of his favourite parts of the song. This method of working, Thom bringing in the initial ideas for the band to then develop, seems to be fairly typical at this point in Radiohead's career. Adding colour and detail and fresh perspectives to something per se is relatively easy (step forward prog rock and twenty minute organ solos!). Doing so without detracting from or forgetting what you had in the first place is a rare gift.

Finally, asked about the politics of the song by *Select* in 1995, Thom gave a delicious and very prescient answer; "We operate like the UN. You can get the veto, but I'm definitely America."

07 JUST

In contrast to the spiritual overtones of the previous track, "Just" is a decidedly secular affair. It opens with a particularly memorable first line – "Can't get the stink off, it's been hanging round for days" – that sets the seedy scene perfectly.

Variously described by Thom as "a competition between me and Jonny to get as many chords as possible into a song" and, to Mac Randall, as "like writing a medley", this ever-changing track has an effervescent Hendrix/early Bowie feel to it. A genuine exuberance and sense of enormous pleasure permeates the whole song. "Just" was the first successful recording from the tortured RAK sessions, which maybe explains the sense of fun.

Although the solid, funky rhythm section and Thom's throat-scraping vocals are outstanding, the highlight of this track is definitely the remarkable guitar playing. In choice, contrasts, voicing and usage of different guitar parts, "Just" is evocative of albums like *Electric Ladyland*, particularly in the "jump cutting" between wildly different guitar parts. It's not easy to be tasteful, challenging, entertaining and exciting all at once, but the band – and particularly Jonny – manage it here.

Many signature Radiohead guitar elements are floating around in the midst of this salty six-string chowder, though several are developed to heights not heard in their music before. To take only the most obvious and literal example, Jonny's rising guitar line, frenetically (and on several occasions dangerously) picked in octaves as it drives the intro along and provides the backdrop to the chorus, is a musical trademark we've heard a number of times before from the band.

A lot of the song's period atmosphere comes from the distinctive modal harmony used (e.g. in the intro). This comes from tightly holding the same chord shape on the guitar and gamely moving it up and down the neck, independent of conventional harmonic concerns. That's why so many of the chords move in recurring patterns (often adjoining note to adjoining note) and are of exactly similar types. There's a chunky, solid physicality about this type of harmony (that can also be heard in the modal jazz pioneered by Miles Davis, in various forms of folk music and in the classical composer Igor Stravinsky's "Rite Of Spring") that makes it really exciting.

The lyrics are somewhat incidental, and don't quite engage the attention (there's probably too much guitar playing going on!). "Just'"is another of Thom's "lecturing songs" (harking back to "How Do You?") and the unfortunate recipient is berated for a lack of integrity and the dire consequences of being "taken in" by something. The opening acoustic guitar riff and its distinctive drum break are surely too similar to "Smells Like Teen Spirit" to be a coincidence, though, particularly after the years of Nirvana comparisons that he band endured.

The song's "early 70/early 90s" musical period was a particularly fertile time for rock star drug deaths, but whether or not the song is directly about Kurt (and/or Hendrix and/or the legions of other rock'n'roll drug casualties) isn't clear. That said, the fact that Thom finishes the song screaming "Why do you do it to yourself? You stupid...." seem pretty telling.

Although hardly conventional chart fodder, as the album's fourth single the track reached number 17 in the UK singles chart, a full seven months after *The Bends* was released – an impressive performance.

08 MY IRON LUNG

"Oh, you mean the one that sounds like Nirvana!" This was the most common reaction that this track elicited among listeners – and it's interesting to investigate why.

There's certainly no denying that "My Iron Lung" does have more than a little of Nirvana about it (opening guitar break, chugging bass line, melodic and harmonic gestures, Nirvana/Pixies-style soft verse/loud chorus dynamics, incomprehensible octave-leaping lyrics in the middle, etc). For much of its length, the song could be "Heart Shaped Box"'s more sophisticated and refined younger brother (or indeed sister, which somehow suits it better): the sibling with the jazz records, the Hendrix, the early Queen and the copy of *Meddle*.

However, we know enough about Radiohead and their musical prowess by now to realize that this didn't come about by accident – so what were they up to? The root of the answer can be found in one word: "Creep".

"My Iron Lung" was written in late 1993, after they had spent a gruelling time promoting "Creep" and *Pablo Honey*, and the band had obviously been feeling the strain, not least because the rewards of all their hard work (*Pablo Honey* went US gold on September 1, 1993) actually seemed to make things worse. "Our so-called success in America...allowed us to do lots of things," Thom told *Q* magazine, "but it also meant that somehow we owed somebody something. But I couldn't work out who, and I couldn't work out how much."

Eventually, tired of being seen as one-hit wonders for "Creep" and of also being declared successors to Nirvana, Radiohead decided to kill off two birds with one stone. If people wanted Radiohead to be the "new Nirvana" then that was what, for one song only and couched in venomously caustic irony, they were going to get. When Thom declared that "My Iron Lung" was meant to be the "final nail in the coffin... of the previous song that shall remain nameles", he was referring to "Creep" and probably also making a sly reference to "Smells Like Teen Spirit". Kurt Cobain famously felt as trapped by that song as Radiohead did by their own millstone. So, how do you set about trying to out-Nirvana Nirvana?

For a start, "My Iron Lung" is a song that manages to trash not only itself and its predecessor ("This is our new song, just like the last one, a total waste of time, my iron lung") but also Radiohead themselves ("Too cynical to speak, we're losing, can't you tell?") and all the new fans that they're so arduously on tour trying to win over in the first place ("Suck, suck your teenage thumb, toilet trained

"Success in America ...allowed us to do lots of things."

and dumb, when the power runs out, we'll just hum"). Then, as if to emphasise the point even more, the band refer to "Creep" as nothing less than a malfunctioning life support system, which is giving them pain by frustratingly enveloping and artistically paralysing them.

The title, of course, is a reference to the cumbersome, claustrophobic and slightly horrific mechanical breathing devices needed by those whose lungs are too weak to work unaided. Along with the track "The Bends", this is the album's most explicit use of medical imagery to evoke dysfunction (a device also used on "Bones" and in the plastic surgery described on "Fake Plastic Trees").

In a strange echo of "Creep", the track would also end up being recorded more or less live after attempts to produce a satisfactory version at the RAK sessions had failed. With the main exception of the lead vocal, which was redone later, "My Iron Lung" was basically recorded from the stage of the band's videoed London Astoria gig on May 27, 1994.

Amazingly enough, given the song's caustically ironic content, it was decided that it would be released as the first single off *The Bends*. It was a big hit with fans and on college radio but spectacularly failed to repeat the success of "Creep", only reaching number 24 in the UK and selling barely 20,000 copies in the US. The band now no longer had to worry about living up to all that high expectation. Now they could just get on with the business of being Radiohead.

09 BULLET PROOF...I WISH I WAS

When a hitherto electric rock band begin writing lots of reflective acoustic songs, it's generally a sure sign that they're been spending too long on the road (all those lonely hours to fill in interchangeable Hyatts and Hiltons). When "Bullet Proof… I Wish I Was", the fourth and most desolate acoustic song on the album, was written, Radiohead appear to have been in desperate need of some time off: "Limb by limb and tooth by tooth, tearing up inside of me/Every day, every hour, wish that I was bullet proof."

As well as the palpable weariness in Thom's voice and Phil's exhausted drumming, the tired resignation is made more acute by the unnatural slowness of the song's melody. Though very similar to "High and Dry" in many respects (broadly the same speed/tempo, similar chords and the same kind of "talking" verse and "soaring" chorus) the melody of "Bullet Proof" is slowed down to a Mogadon-zapped half-speed relative to the rest of the song. Taken together with the words, the sense is very much that of a tranquillised, post-anxiety-attack haze.

This feeling of pharmaceutically-induced calm is reinforced by the amazing wash of ambient guitar noises that envelop the song like a fog from the outset. It's the kind of simple song/strange noise juxtaposition that's been used many times by such, um, notable non-drug takers as Jimi Hendrix, The Velvet Underground, early Floyd, Gong, Hawkwind, and more recently Spiritualized.

In all psychedelia, the listener tends to decode this aural picture by assuming that the tune represents the singer's conscious thoughts, whilst the background melee describes his corresponding subconscious ones. This effect was to become increasingly common in Radiohead's future work. It wasn't originally planned quite that artfully, though.

As with the similar and, paradoxically, more grounded "High and Dry", the song's backing track (acoustic guitar, bass and drums) was initially recorded by Thom, Colin and Phil, and seemed almost perfectly complete in itself. Which, in a band of three guitarists, obviously raises a question: what's left for Ed and Jonny to do that will make the song better rather than worse?

After working out Jonny's pretty Johnny Marr-meets-Neil Young guitar figure, the band weren't really sure what to do. The golden rule in a recording studio is, "If in doubt, make noise," so they decided to run a whole load of guitars through a whole load of pedals. Jonny has called it "the old Pink Floyd trick" and, moreover, just to guarantee a suitably ambient result, it was decided they'd do it without hearing the track they were supposedly accompanying.

Ed O'Brien was a tad suspicious at first. "I remember thinking, 'Bastards –- I've never recorded like this before. How are you supposed to do it?'" he recalls on the Radiohead interview disc. Nonetheless, the process produced some fabulous material. Jonny has often cited Floyd's *Meddle* as an influence and there is definitely more than an echo of that album in the elemental calls and sculptural constructions on "Bullet Proof".

Post-editing and arranging, Radiohead arrived at a thoroughly musical, very lovely tone poem of pure guitar. In its final form, with the rest of the band floating gently and "unplugged" in its midst, the song's various elements complement each other wonderfully.

10 BLACK STAR

"Repeat and fade" may be a commonplace way of ending a track, but it's a most unusual way to begin one. In fact, the only other example I can recall is Boston's "More Than A Feeling", hardly a terribly appropriate comparison point.

Nevertheless, this is how "Black Star" begins, and as if to heighten the strangeness, something is making the needle stick in the proverbial groove. Although the music wants to move on with its story, it's held back, forced to chase its own tail and ultimately getting nowhere. The whole song is essentially encapsulated in a bar-and-a-half.

The central, striking lyrical theme of "Black Star", the breakdown of a suburban relationship as a symptom of cosmic malady, isn't one you often come across in the average pop ditty. Rather it's a specific combination you much more readily associate with T.S. Eliot works such as *The Hollow Men* or *The Love Song Of J. Alfred Prufrock*. The fact that three of Radiohead majored in English makes it likely that these poems exerted an influence, even if it was only a subconscious one.

Eliot and Radiohead have both tapped into the same archetypal ways of expressing concern about man's place in the universe and the meaning of life. Even the image of the black star itself (a unseen anti-sun which radiates negativity and malevolence into the universe) is hardly new: it even formed a staple of the medieval mystery plays. However, it's fascinating to observe the place it takes in Thom's vivid lyrical landscape of impotent motorcycle stuntmen, fake Chinese rubber plants, failing iron lungs and sociable answerphones.

The song's lyrics relate a harrowing tale about a domestic relationship in serious trouble. It's essentially a kitchen-sink drama about an overstretched man slowly falling out of love with the mentally fragile partner who relies on him. Thom is well known to be a fan of Scott Walker, and "Black Star" has a similar bittersweet mix of the painful and the uplifting. It's a sad, sweet aural sunset. *Pablo Honey*'s "Vegetable' deals with a similar scenario, but "Black Star" is in a different league entirely. The lyrical detail is far more inventive. We learn of a dressing gown worn all day, and the fact that it's exactly 58 hours since the man last slept with his partner. These touching, acutely observed real life details make the story that much more credible and powerfully engage the listener's emotions. The protagonist's frustrations are similarly mirrored in the monotonous, repetitive music.

Against this, the chorus is both a relief and a contrast. Much more declamatory, it's both a gritting of the teeth and a shrug of the shoulders as Yorke looks for an answer to why things go wrong: "The Black Star... the falling sky... the satellite that beams me home". As certainties crumble, the angry distorted guitars that have been quietly shadowing the vocal seethe gleefully to the front.

It's a surprise to learn that such a "heavy" number was recorded in a state of jokey high spirits when John Leckie was away from of the studio. Johnny Greenwood has described a real "Teacher's away larkiness" to the day it was recorded, going on to praise the track's "ace raggedness."

There remains something undeniably positive to "Black Star" which is down to much more than just the minor-to-major key change in the chorus. The track has an indomitability and self-belief, an unshakeable confidence that things will somehow turn out all right. The sun may be setting now, but it will definitely rise again in the morning. Produced by Radiohead and Nigel Godrich, "Black Star" was to be the first product of a very fruitful and enduring partnership.

11 SULK

"Sulk" was originally one of the front-runners in the quest for a hit single to follow "Creep". It was only finally put to tape at the very end of the Abbey Road sessions, and one can only imagine how fed up with it the band must have been by then. Yet you certainly wouldn't know it from the performance, which is as forceful and energetic as any track on the album. The track begins in trip-hop land, all ambient reverbs, jazz-soul drums and dub guitar weirdness. Almost immediately, however, this pattern is completely subverted by some drip-drop guitar arpeggios towing a conversational bass run, and straightaway we're rattling and humming our way through probably the most U2-like song that Radiohead have ever recorded.

The lyrics are as baleful as you might expect in a song called "Sulk", but Thom's supremely Bono-like vocal performance is nonetheless uplifting. Though things get stirred up in the nicely key-shifted middle guitar section, the song basically wouldn't be out of place on *The Joshua Tree* (where else was a tambourine ever heard in a Radiohead song, for example?). As the Hammond organ kicks in, it's difficult to shake off mental images of a gold-lamé suited T. Yorke driving through Las Vegas vainly looking for a good bookshop.

It's no crime. All artists occasionally try on new hats, experiment with different styles and directions, and here Radiohead don U2's ten gallon titfers and stretch themselves – upwards, in the case of Thom's vocals. "Groove" is not a word greatly associated with Radiohead, but that's essentially what this song is about – stripping things down to a basic groove, and locking in together as a band. And, thanks to two years of more or less constant playing, they lock in superbly. "Sulk" swings along gamely, and Colin Greenwood in particular obviously enjoys his new space and flexibility.

12 STREET SPIRIT (FADE OUT)

The fifth and last track off *The Bends* to be given a single release (on September 22, 1996) and that some 10 months after the album itself, "Street Spirit (Fade Out)" unexpectedly became Radiohead's most successful UK single so far, reaching an impressive number 5 in the singles charts. Like fellow album-closers "Blow Out" (*Pablo Honey*) and "The Tourist" (*OK Computer*), it's a strikingly different track to the rest of album, hence the possible appeal to otherwise non-Radiohead loving record buyers.

'Street Spirit" is the nearest Radiohead have come so far on this album fully political song. With its twangy electric folk guitars to the fore, it bemoans man's seemingly insatiable appetite for environmental and personal destruction. Despite this, poetics rather than polemics are the song's focus, and lyrically "Street Spirit" is far more akin to the cappuccino introspection of REM, Joni Mitchell or Paul Simon than it is to any clarion-call rabble-rousing.

This track an early sign of Radiohead's burgeoning political awareness, and further evidence of their lyrical maturing and broader worldview. It's difficult to imagine the swooning emotional pressure cooker of "You" or "Creep" finding the mental space for such thoughts, and it shows the distance the band had already travelled by the time they wrote this song in late 1993. Yet henceforth, such "big issue" songs and statements would be an increasingly prominent feature of their output.

Each verse of the lyric has a slightly different lyrical style and subject matter to contrast with the recurring refrain, "and fade out again and fade out" (again). In the course of thirteen lines they career from surreal suburban menace through astonishingly positive (for Radiohead) New Age-isms ("Be a world child, form a circle before we all go under" and "Immerse your soul in love") to morbidly freaked-out expressionism. The constantly changing, but

consistently vivid, imagery once again keeps the listener hooked. The lyrical repetition of the refrain has a rhetorical, if extremely subtle, parallel with the musical repetition of the introduction.

Musically, it's interesting how one passage (the twanging electric guitar arpeggios) can suggest a number of styles and periods simultaneously. In this particular case, a ("peace man") two fingers of 60s protest/West Coast folk-rock, a good dollop of spaghetti western (Ennio Morricone would be an important influence on *OK Computer*), a jigger of 70s country-rock and a pinch of 80/90s indie music all come to mind.

These elements hold together in a cogent and enjoyable way because they're all tightly derived from the same piece of generative material, the descending three-note motif of the refrain: Fade, Out, A(gain). It's a not-so-slight return to "Planet Telex".

Last, but by no means least, are the band really going to be so literal as to fade out a piece entitled "(Fade out)"? With only 30 seconds to go, after using more or less the same glacially repeating chord sequence (C, Em, Am) for the entire piece, it appears likely. Then suddenly, for the words "Immerse (yourself in love)" , Team Radiohead make a (chord) substitution – G for C – and hit the back of the musical net. It's a very tasty climax, artfully throwing the rest of the song into relief, and providing the emotional hiatus from where it can be brought gently to an (artistically) safe stop.

OK COMPUTER
1997

Though *The Bends* was initially a slow seller in the US (it peaked at number 88 in the album charts) it had consolidated Radiohead's critical reputation mightily. In the rest of the world, the critical plaudits were no less extravagant but the band managed to sell a few records too. The album was a classic word-of-mouth success, and in the next six months sold 500,000 copies in the UK alone.

On one level, of course, it was marvellous that the band were a huge commercial success. However, it meant that when Radiohead came to think about recording their next album, they were not only facing the same problem of satisfying expectations that had so nearly derailed *The Bends*, they were doing it with considerably raised stakes and under even harsher public scrutiny

The recording of *The Bends* had been so traumatic, threatening to tear the band apart at one stage, that a repeat of that working method just couldn't be countenanced. Another way had to be found.

Desperate to avoid being trapped by a conventional studio environment, and having hit it off with engineer and soon to be co-producer Nigel Godrich while recording *The Bends*, they asked him to assemble a mobile set-up which they could take wherever they liked.

As Thom told *Mojo* magazine, "We were nostalgic for the time when Jonny and I used to do 4-track stuff...do it when we felt like it, go round his house, write a song, tape it and fuck off home. That's what we were trying to do here."

Thus the dynamism, spontaneity and freedom that Radiohead so enjoyed when they played live could be transferred into the studio.

Before the success of "Creep" had turned their world on its head, Radiohead had been more or less quietly enjoying a comfortable, even privileged, middle class lifestyle. In the England of the 1990s, the rock business had become a respectable

middle class profession in the way that acting had half a century earlier (in Britain, as everywhere else, respectability follows the money), and while they were undoubtedly as passionate and as professional as they could be about their music, there was still something about Radiohead of the "Gentleman Amateur".

"Creep" and what followed changed all that, propelling them breathlessly into the neon maw of the American rock machine. It sharpened them up and tuned them into professionals all right, but initially it left them winded and hurting too – hence the violent reaction of *The Bends*. Time heals all wounds though, and by the time *The Bends* was actually released in March 1995 they were already becoming accustomed to their new life. As they began to write new material for what would become *OK Computer*, they were beginning to "catch up" with themselves, reassessing themselves and their music in the light of their experience and new place in the world.

As Radiohead progressed with their heavy schedule over the next year, constantly touring and writing, it was natural enough to start combining the two activities. The band began testing their new songs out on their own and, as support act on tours by REM (the 1995 Monster tour), Soul Asylum and Alanis Morissette, other people's audiences.

Hearing the new material for the first time live, and even more so in an arena context, the band's American record company, Capitol, was delighted, foreseeing a hugely successful, i.e. best-selling, new album of readily digestible crowd-pleasers. What they eventually got when the band went into the studio in mid-summer 1996 was rather different.

"We'd been listening to Ennio Morricone and Can and lots of stuff where they're abusing the recording process," Thom was later to tell *Mojo*. "We wanted to try that." They didn't have to wait long for results. Having set the studio up and turned it on, the very first take they recorded was, bar a few touch-ups, the final version of "No Surprises".

That the band could achieve such a result so quickly tells you that fundamentally they already had a sure sense of who they were, and what they wanted to achieve. Naturally, there were teething troubles as the band acclimatized to their environment, but without the time pressures and conventions of a normal studio to restrict them and with the ironically titled "No Surprises" as a stunningly positive starting point, they set off on a voyage of discovery.

Along the way this spirit of exploration would extend to Radiohead taking the studio out of the familiar surroundings of their Oxfordshire rehearsal space, an ex-apple shed excruciatingly dubbed "Canned Applause", and following their muse up the M4 to the rather more palatial surroundings of St. Catherine's Court, a 15th-Century mansion near Bath belonging to the actress Jane Seymour.

One by one the potential arena hits that had so cheered the record execs fell away.

More ambitious and yet at the same time more successful than anything they had produced before, *OK Computer* is the product of a band supremely at ease with itself. The individually glittering, somewhat schizoid faces of *The Bends*, as well as its youthful nervous excitement, have been honed, reabsorbed, augmented and polished into a smoother, more profound and deeply alluring whole. Both freer and more consistent, it is a work of compelling maturity.

When finally released (in the UK on June 16, 1997, and in the US on July 1), the album was rapturously received, despite the worst fears of the band's initially bemused US record company. Swiftly becoming Radiohead's first UK number 1 album, it also revived their fortunes in the US where it peaked at a respectable number 21. But that was only the beginning. Topping many end-of-year polls and winning a string of awards (including a Grammy for "Best Alternative Rock Performance"), it sent the band's critical and popular reputation into the stratosphere.

In February 1998, eight months after the album's release, the readers of *Q*, the UK's biggest selling music magazine, voted *OK Computer* the best album of all time. In the magazine's 15th Anniversary poll of September 2001, some three-and-a-half years later and an aeon in traditional pop music terms, they were still doing the same.

The *Sunday Telegraph*'s James Delingpole gave the album the following assessment: "If *The Bends* was the best album of the 1990s, *OK Computer* is surely the finest of the 21st century." A tad ambitious perhaps, but he's yet to be proved wrong

01 AIRBAG

As critical plaudits greeted *The Bends*, Thom Yorke had found himself increasingly irritated by one thing in particular. Feeling that the critics had wrongly stereotyped all the band's songs as miserable, he determined to do something about it: "We could really fall back on just doing another moribund, miserable, morbid and negative record...but I really don't want to, at all. And I'm deliberately just writing down all the positive things that I hear or see." But he admitted to *NME* in December 1995: "I'm not able to put them into music yet."

OK Computer, Thom Yorke told *Launch* magazine, is "not really about computers, it was just the noise that was going on in my head for most of the year and a half of travelling, and computers and television and just absorbing it all." Miles Davis' *Bitches Brew* and The Beatles' "White" album were obviously swimming about as major influences. The Beach Boys, Johnny Cash and Morricone were somewhere around too, but holding his own with the big boys was LA "illbient" trip-hop guru DJ Shadow. The combination of Radiohead, Thom's new positivity, DJ Shadow and a longstanding suspicion of cars is where the album begins with "Airbag".

"Airbag" was jointly inspired by Sogyal Rinpoche's *The Tibetan Book Of Living And Dying* and a headline Thom saw in an automobile magazine: "An Airbag Saved My Life". Thom had been in a car crash just after sitting his final school exams and, famously able to harbour a grudge, had been wary of cars and transportation in general ever since.

As Thom explained to *Time Out*: "Nothing scares me more than driving, I hate it with a fucking passion. I hate it because it's the most dangerous thing you do in your life. Your average expensive German car gives you the feeling that you can't die. And that's a fraud. Really, when you think about it, every time you get home you should run down the street screaming 'I'm back! I'm alive!' "

Thom takes this obsession one stage further in the lyric to "Airbag", where a transportation crash becomes a redeeming, almost Christ-like experience: "In a jack-knifed juggernaut I am born again... In an intastella burst I am back to save the universe!"

It's a theme he later revisits in "Lucky", and musically too there are many ideas, figures and textures introduced in "Airbag" that will feature throughout the rest of

OK Computer, giving the whole collection a terrific cohesion. To give a few examples, the ecstatic feeling of both vocal and music anticipate a prevalent dreamy (and sometimes nightmarish) quality throughout the album. The "stream of consciousness" we saw in tracks like the "The Bends" and "Bullet Proof" has burst its banks and flooded this entire album, with almost every track given a thorough soaking in the process.

The busy shiny guitar part, meanwhile, introduces a melodic fragment (three descending then oscillating notes) that will in one way or another recur again and again throughout the album ("Subterranean Homesick Alien", "Let Down", "No Surprises", etc.)

Lyrically, too, there is a similar sense of focusing inwards while gazing outwards (or vice versa) throughout much of the album. The "Creep" of *Pablo Honey* has lifted his gaze from himself, through his immediate vicinity (*The Bends*) to the wider world around him, but at the same time we perceive his thoughts and feelings in a more acute way. Thom's lyrics are more reactive and more experiential, more observational and yet metaphorical than ever before.

The whole of "Airbag" is crammed with acute musical detail: the opening "brown" guitar line, for example, (often cited as reminiscent of Robert Fripp's opening line on King Crimson's "Red"), and the sensitive way it's doubled with the cello. Then there's Colin's spare and groovy bass line, the multiple guitar textures, the musical use of effects and ambience, and many, many other devices.

One of the most famous features of the song is its crunchy, squashy drum part. The work of DJ Shadow and his contemporaries (Tricky et al) had already influenced the drum part of "Street Spirit" B-side "Talk Show Host", but this was the first time (with the arguable exception of "Planet Telex") that it had surfaced on an album. The track was made by sampling fragments of Phil's playing which were then programmed up and passed through Jonny's guitar pedals (his amazingly monikered "Lovetone Meatball" filter pedal, by the sound of it).

All of this sonic abuse is very reminiscent of 70s German band Can, another significant influence on the album. As Thom enthused to Mac Randall, "They always used to do their own stuff, and they were in a big room with bits of blankets and beds and shit, and Holger Czukay would endlessly, endlessly tape, tape, tape, and then splice it together. It just sounded such an amazingly cool thing to do. Basically four-track gone berserk."

The US-only EP "Airbag/How Am I Driving" was released in April 1998, and debuted at number 56 the same week that *OK Computer* went platinum there.

As a final "motoring" postscript, Thom would complete a circle of influences in June 1997 by collaborating with DJ Shadow on the spooky "Rabbit In Your Headlights" track of UNKLE's 1998 album *Psyence Fiction*.

02 PARANOID ANDROID

Along with "Creep", "Paranoid Android" is probably Radiohead's most famous song. It's an emotionally volatile, musically supple, multi-part epic that is often referred to as being in the great tradition of The Beatles' "A Day In The Life", Queen's "Bohemian Rhapsody" and Led Zeppelin's "Stairway to Heaven". The closest ancestors in Radiohead's previous output are the also multi-sectional "road diary" of "The Bends" and the electric effervescence of "Just", highlights of the band's preceding album. That said, neither has the "Paranoid Android" persuasive grandeur. Both songs make great use of "jump cutting", and the genesis of "Paranoid Android" really lies in the band simply wanting to have more fun with something they already enjoyed doing.

The idea of "Paranoid Android" started to take shape when Thom walked into rehearsal one day and suggested the band write a song along the lines of the Beatles' "Happiness Is A Warm Gun", which is essentially three songs put together. With its vaguely sinister lyric, acoustic intro, choral midsection, acid electric guitars and complicated twists and turns, the Beatles' song does make a fair blueprint, but at only 2" 43" it's still a bit on the short side. Undeterred, they set to work to pack the song with as many disparate elements as possible.

A few months later, with the process of musical construction well underway,

Thom told *Q* magazine that he had an encounter in an LA bar which determined the song's lyrical direction, and in particular spawned the "kicking screaming Gucci little piggy" line. He saw somebody spill a drink over a woman: "She turned into this fiend. There was a look in her eyes that I'd never ever seen before... everyone was out of their minds on coke. I just saw her face, and thought, 'Fucking hell what was that?'" Thom was more direct to *Time Out*: " 'Paranoid Android' is about the dullest fucking people on Earth."

In suitably cynical spirit, the title given to the song refers to "Marvin", the tiresome, self-righteous and depressive robot from Douglas Adams' *Hitchhiker's Guide to The Galaxy*.

"If you think it's a long song now, you should have heard it then," Ed O'Brien told Followmearound.com. "It was eight to ten minutes longer, and when we started playing it live, it was completely hilarious. There was a rave section and a Hammond organ outro, and we'd be pissing ourselves while we played. We'd bring out the glockenspiel and it would be really, really funny." Not surprisingly these elements were dropped when it came time to record the song in Jane Seymour's mansion.

"Paranoid Android" is more complex than "Bohemian Rhapsody" or "Stairway to Heaven" which are genuine three-part epics in the sense that all three parts are different. The dynamics and speed shifts of "Paranoid Android" are different too. "Stairway" and "Bohemian Rhapsody" both have slow starts, faster, more expansive middle sections and still faster "head-banging" finales. "Paranoid Android" starts and ends at the same tempo with similar material and has a slower chorale in the middle.

"Paranoid Android" is in some ways more along the A-B-A model of "A Day In The Life" or even more so classical sonata form, in that the first A section further contains various "nested" subsections: real and transformed repetitions, developed bridge passages etc. It's a very clever piece of work, reminiscent on a grand scale of the way the band invigorate the deceptively simple "Lucky".

The basic premise of the song is an alternately oblique and cruelly specific condemnation of the loathsome, coke-snorting little piggy/yuppies mentioned in the song's mid-sections. Thom's pained reference at the start to the "unborn chicken voices in my head" keeping him awake is very reminiscent of his general comments about *OK Computer* previously quoted in the "Airbag" section. The Latin rhythmic feel of the opening and closing sections is also interesting as it's hardly a Radiohead staple. Thom's delicate acoustic intro, Ed's virtuoso clave playing, Jonny's space guitar and the Dark Side Of The Moon "I'm not frightened of dying"-style mumblings are also worth an aural photo.

Moving along to the pejorative "Gucci little piggy" sub-section we have a nifty and unsettling change of metre (to 7/8 – seven quicker beats in a bar), ominous 50s guitar pickings and tasteful Fender Rhodes sneaking in under the curtain before the first strummed tremolo/Brian May guitar maelstrom heralds Thom picking up his executioner's axe. There's a lovely harmonic change from the minor to major here, spinning things round to close the first section.

Lyrically, it's not entirely clear what happens here but one gets the impression that after Thom's heartfelt, "Rain down" calls for cleansing, he sensibly decides to kick pork butt and the piggies (a reference perhaps to Lennon's "White" album swine) finally get their comeuppance: "That's it sir, you're leaving, the crackle of pig skin, the dust and the screaming...God loves his children".

After the tension of the first section this "chorale" is a welcome relief. The pressure cooker lid goes well and truly back on though for the wildly filtered (an aural link to "Airbag") closing guitar reprise which winds everything up nicely in more ways than one, before pulling the plug. This guarantees a huge feeling of relief at the start of "Subterranean Homesick Alien" connecting the tracks and further tightening the album's sense of coherence.

Released on May 26, 1997 as an unlikely "it'll never get any radio play" single to

"...she turned into this fiend..."

lead off the album, "Paranoid Android" proved the pundits wrong in style. Swiftly reaching number 3 in the UK singles chart it remains the band's most successful ever British single.

03 SUBTERRANEAN HOMESICK ALIEN

Originally entitled "Uptight", the title given to the track as it's found on *OK Computer* is an obvious allusion to Bob Dylan's classic "Subterranean Homesick Blues", a cheeky bit of punning and an elegant bit of internal rhyming. Though quite different in effect, the two songs share an obvious parallel in their "stream of consciousness" agenda. Radiohead's take on reverie is extremely naturalistic, as was previously seen on "[Nice Dream]" and "Bullet Proof". With all that languid vocal, dreamy Rhodes piano and swooshing psychedelic guitar swirling around, it's not difficult to imagine yourself flying through fluffy clouds of neurons in Thom Yorke's head.

Many people have commented on the psychedelic feel of "Subterranean Homesick Alien" evoking Pink Floyd's "Great Gig In The Sky" or The Beatles' "Lucy In The Sky With Diamonds". It certainly has many similarities, not least in its sense of space. Radiohead's track doesn't jump awake (by changing metre) in the chorus, though: it just turns over and carries on snoozing.

Thom described the track to *Launch* as a "joke song": ("As much as my jokes are ever funny") with the lyrics inspired by an old essay question from Abingdon: "You are an alien from another planet. You've landed and you're standing in the middle of Oxford. What do you see?"

The nub of the story is Thom's childhood confusion involving angels and aliens. As he confessed to *Options* magazine in 1998: "I just loved the idea of someone observing how we live from the outside...sitting there pissing themselves laughing at how humans go about their daily business." This, without the laughter and incontinence, is exactly what the aliens of the song's title are up to: observing and sending reports back home. The song's "uptight" protagonist watches the "uptight" aliens, wishing he could be "rescued" by them and taken away from his humdrum everyday life.

The subtext of all this is misplaced spirituality, and most pertinently that invested in UFO theories of the "Was God An Astronaut?" variety. As Jonny told *Launch*: "Before UFOs it was the Virgin Mary...and before that it was something else. People just flock to the same places with their cameras, and hope to see the same things. And it's just about hope and faith, I think, more than aliens." From someone who is the subject of no small amount of mass adulation and interest himself, it's an interesting perspective. The song is actually the oldest on the album, having been written during the *The Bends* sessions and for a long time was played live by Thom and Jonny as an acoustic duo. They didn't quite know how to take it any further until they hit on the sound of the Fender Rhodes (played on the track by Thom) and made a link to Miles Davis.

As Thom told *Q* in October 1997, " 'Subterranean Homesick Alien' was born out of listening to (Miles Davis' 1969 album) *Bitches Brew* endlessly every time I drove my car...The first time I heard it I thought it was the most nauseating chaos. I felt sick listening to it. Then gradually [there's] something incredibly brutal about it and something incredibly beautiful ...you're never quite sure where you are in it, it seems to be swimming around you. It has that sound of a huge empty space, like a cathedral. It wasn't jazz and it didn't sound like rock'n'roll. It was building something up and watching it fall apart, that's the beauty of it. It was at the core of what we were trying to do with *OK Computer*...I completely missed it, but then again I didn't."

I would certainly say he didn't. As well as being a marvellous description of both *Bitches Brew* and latterly "Subterranean Homesick Alien" it's a very cogent analysis of what's happening under the skin of all the tracks on *OK Computer*.

As well as having some of the textures freedom and airiness of *Bitches Brew* (which let's not forget was a profound influence on early Floyd too), there are other qualities about the track, such as its delicate buoyancy, poignant lyricism and perky rhythmic drive, that have more to do with the earlier Davis of *Miles Ahead* and *Sketches Of Spain* as well as John Coltrane's *A Love Supreme*. The rasping experimentalism and hard edged sonic science of *Bitches Brew* that so initially baffled Thom would eventually be echoed on *Kid A*.

In its original 1957 liner notes, Nat Hentoff describes *Miles Ahead* as "a compelling blend of the 'deep song' of flamenco and the cry of the blues". Wind the clock forward thirty-eight years, factor in the history of rock music, and you have "Subterranean Homesick Alien" and *OK Computer*.

There is another comparison to be drawn with Miles and his contemporaries. With their earnest approach and appetite for musical exploration, Radiohead may sometimes seem quaintly out of step with today's music scene, but they would feel right at home in 1950's New York. Are Radiohead really the be-boppers of the 21st century, and *OK Computer* a re-rebirth of the Cool?

04 EXIT MUSIC (FOR A FILM)

B minor is, according to Spinal Tap's Nigel Smalls, "the saddest of keys". If you had any lingering doubts about Nigel's wisdom, banish them now as we turn to "Exit Music (For a Film)" the most heart wrenching song on a far from flippant album. If "Fitter Happier"'s desolation is the result of an absence of emotions, this song bursts like a rain cloud with them: love, hope, fear, anger, hatred. It's an amazing journey to make in just over four minutes.

Thom recalled the track in *Mojo* as "the first performance we'd ever recorded where every note of it made my head spin – something I was proud of, something I could turn up really loud and not wince at any moment."

The band intended the track to sound like Ennio Morricone, and it does have something of the overwrought, vastly reverbed acoustic guitar and choir constructions of his spaghetti western period. *For a Few Dollars More* comes particularly to mind, with the band's sustained, distorted bass and soaring, appropriately ghostly guitar substituting for Morricone's church organ.

The song was written specifically for Baz Luhrman's brilliant 1996 re-imagining of Shakespeare's *Romeo & Juliet*, and it's story is that of the star-crossed young lovers. The track was heard over the film's final credits, meaning that it was the first song from *OK Computer* that the public got to hear, after the previously-released "Lucky".

The song's protagonists are initially preparing to steal away: "Wake from your dreams..." They intend to escape in the early morning: "before all hell breaks loose". However, a crisis of nerve ensues: "Breathe, keep breathing/Don't loose your nerve". Then tragedy develops: "You can laugh a spineless laugh, we hope your rules and wisdom choke you/Now we are one in everlasting peace, we hope that you choke, that you choke." It's devastating stuff, made all the more so by one of Thom Yorke's very best vocal performances: first fragile, then frightened, then raging.

An important motif of the performance, lyric and arrangement is breath and air. With it life, without it death. In the lyric meanwhile the journey from "Wake" to "Breathe" to "Sing" to "Laugh" to "Choke" is a précis of the doomed young lovers' final bleak journey.

A less tangible but no less significant contributor to the song's effect is the desiccated, tomb-like ambience enclosing Thom's vocals. The sound is very dry: parched as if his lips are stuck together. Throwing his voice into sharp relief against the lonely guitar, the room's decay seems to pick out his consonants (waKkke, sleePpp, escaPppe paCcKk) and we get a vivid sense of his imprisonment by family politics and physical environment, equally ready to close

down on him and deprive him of breath at any moment. As Thom told *Q*, it was a quite deliberate effect.

"If you listen to the rhythm at the beginning of 'Exit Music' it starts off like a Johnny Cash song from his prison tapes [*Johnny Cash At Folsom Prison* and *Johnny Cash At San Quentin*]. It's amazing. I hate live albums but I get spine tingles every time I play that. You can hear the audience willing him on. And you can hear he's ill, he can't hit the notes and yet the songs are so powerful in that environment with the prisoners there. 'Exit Music' came about from trying to get a similar sound to that album."

The vocal was recorded in the stone hallway of St Catherine's Court, and written with the space specifically in mind. It is reminiscent of the post-party "Planet Telex" studio jam, but in a far more rarefied and finely drawn way. The song finally chokes out on a sadly ironic B major chord.

05 LET DOWN

Thom Yorke has a problem with sentimentality. The key phrase of "Let Down" is: "Don't get sentimental it always ends up drivel".

As Thom told *Q*: "Sentimentality is being emotional for the sake of it. We're bombarded with sentimentality, people emoting. That's the let down. You end up feeling every emotion is fake, or rather every emotion is on the same plane, whether it's a car advert or a pop song." He's describing the media version of the "fridge buzz" of superficiality and degraded emotional equivalence explored elsewhere on the album ("Karma Police", "Paranoid Android", "Fitter Happier" and "No Surprises"). This very cleverly assembled song is firstly a mirror, than pretty quickly a condemnation of this state of affairs.

The song has a terrific Walker Brothers-join-the-Beach-Boys-and-meet-the-Velvet-Underground-at-the-Factory (Andy Warhol's or Tony Wilson's) feeling to it. The sweet 60s pop versus "tambourines and toms" set-up beloved of the Velvets, Joy Division and so many later 80s bands gives the song a woozy teenage feel. It sounds like we are let down and hanging around the youth club or street corner. Of all the songs on *OK Computer*, this one, recorded live at 3am in the ballroom of St.Catherine's Court, best conforms to Colin and Ed's ideas of Radiohead as "Frank Sinatra meets Joy Division" and "a troubled Phil Spector".

Against a noncommittal musical background, Thom sings his suitably plain, hymn-like verse, just listing transportation trivia as he progresses: "Motorways and tramlines, starting and then stopping".

Thom has said that for him this process represents a "purging" of excess emotion. By the end of the first line he's already starting to heat up emotionally, "taking off and landing".

"We're bombarded with sentimentality, people emoting..."

More layers of ambiguity, this time in the context of the album, are added by the fact that Jonny's initial line is a first cousin of "Airbag", "Subterranean Homesick Alien" and "No Surprises" whilst the rhythm of Thom's verses is exactly the same as "No Surprises". These two songs are strikingly similar in a number of other ways and essentially mirror each other: "Let Down" calls for a greater emotional range, while "No Surprises" is actually praying for less.

The chorus melody is basically the same falling four-note motif that underpins the verse: it's just developed a kink in the middle, and works over two bars rather than eight. The many superimposed layers of metrical, melodic, structural, even contextual equivalence are a fantastic analogue of the "fridge buzz" state of Thom's emotions at this point, providing the background from which he can emerge in the course of the song.

Thom gets progressively more agitated in the second verse: "Shell smash, juices flowing, legs twitch". It implies that his emotions are readying themselves like a newborn butterfly opening its wings. Sure enough, the vocal line then splits in two (very Everly Brothers): a very significant moment, as if we're coming back through the emotional looking glass. Now he can take flight: "One day I'm gonna grow wings, a chemical reaction, hysterical and useless".

Thom starts the third verse before, in an even more extravagant development than previously, an extra voice appears to reprise the second verse while he vamps over the top. It's quite a distance from the song's opening blank descriptions, which is of course entirely the point. "Let Down" is a brilliantly executed, restrained parable of emotional rebirth, hence the song's overall impression of cool euphoria, and is without doubt one of the standout tracks on an already remarkable album.

Right at the song's very end, the chirpy electronics pay a return visit, chattering randomly through the songs melody notes in a vain attempt to mimic the interplay between Jonny and Ed. Though sounding benign, the progression graphically demonstrates that to a machine, the emotional value of all musical notes is exactly the same – nil. It's a neat nod forward to "Fitter Happier"'s more chilling demonstration of the same idea.

06 KARMA POLICE

A deep undercurrent of *OK Computer* is a strain of black surreal comedy. This is mostly discernable as savage irony ("Fitter Happier" and "Paranoid Android') but is also evident in the genuinely humorous and Beatles-esque "Karma Police". Offering some welcome comic relief in between the earnest euphoria of "Let Down" and the ghastliness of "Fitter Happier", the track is one of the album's lightest moments.

The title of this droll outing has its origins in a band in-joke. Jonny Greenwood told *Music Week* magazine in 1997: "It's a favourite saying of ours. Whenever we hear about someone behaving offensively, we say, 'The karma police will catch up with them'."

The particular miscreants of this song have something of the same insensitivity as the piggies of "Paranoid Android", as Thom explained to *Q*: "I get stressed pretty easily and I can't handle having people looking at me in that certain way [acts out curly-lipped malice]. That's what Karma Police and a lot of the album is about. Though it's a joke as well, you know: 'Karma Police, arrest this man.' That's not entirely serious; I hope people will realize that." As the other crimes on the charge sheet include "talking in maths", and being found in possession of "a Hitler hairdo", it would be difficult not to.

The crime of "buzzing like a fridge" and sounding "like a detuned radio" is a more serious charge, however. The often deleterious effects of "noise", particularly that of the psychological and emotional varieties, are a primary theme of *OK Computer*, and one which is referenced in various ways, from the thoughtless background and "unborn chicken" noises of "Paranoid Android" through the emotional static underlying "Let Down" to the terrifying distortions of "Fitter Happier" and "Climbing Up The Walls".

However, in this track Thom's playing mostly for laughs, and the comedy gets funnier as the song progresses. Though always a dramatically aware singer, the pantomime mock-threats of, "This is what you get when you mess with us", and the outrageous vaudeville of, "Phew, for a minute there I lost myself" are without precedent on a Radiohead album.

As well as stealing a number of the Beatles best "White" album period musical jokes (e.g. the exaggerated background sighs) and literally funny noises (e.g. the elephantine guitar noise at the end of the track), Radiohead have picked up on the masters" use of musical and lyrical theatricality. A good example is the chorus, where the hollow threat, "This is what you get when you mess with us" is given far too much of a serious setting by being accompanied by a quasi-religious a cappella choir.

"I can't handle having people looking at me in that certain way"

There is a further layer of humour. "Karma Police" is reminiscent of the Beatles' mid/late-period, and the "White" album's "Sexy Sadie" in particular, in just too many ways (chord progression, melody, instrumental sounds, production etc.) to be accidental. The second you hear that distinctive jangle-piano progression, you're in on the joke. The song isn't just a pastiche and wouldn't be nearly as funny if it was. Radiohead are "clowning" to great effect in the Beatles' distinctive clothes, and even adding to the wardrobe in the way they use modern studio techniques (e.g. the "sampled guitar squeezed through a toothpaste tube" effect at the end) to thoroughly Beatles-like effect.

I'm certain John Lennon would have approved, and the great British public seemed to agree. When released as the second single from the album (August 25, 1997) backed by the suitably bad karma of "Climbing Up The Walls", "Karma Police" stole up the British chart to number 8. The band, as they say in England, were laughing.

07 FITTER HAPPIER

Thom Yorke has said *OK Computer* is not about computers. Given that the most striking feature of this track is its disturbing computer-voice narration and the ironic replacement of the band's singer by a computer, then, we might be justified in asking, what is it about?

Sandwiched in between the relatively upbeat "Karma Police" (which introduces it by way of a "dying" frozen digitised guitar loop) and the defiantly kinetic "Electioneering", "Fitter Happier" is not only the album's central point (more or less), it is also the final descent into desolation. Like Milton's frozen image of hell, it marks *OK Computer*'s emotional nadir.

The voice reading Thom's ironic text is everyday enough, belonging to his Macintosh computer and more specifically its Simple Text application (the one the rest of us delete because we've no possible use for it). Speaking to *Options* magazine in 1998, he was to describe the track as "the most upsetting thing I've ever written. The reason we used a computer voice is that it appeared to be emotionally neutral. In fact it wasn't [neutral], because the inflections that it uses made it – to me – incredibly emotional. It brought out something that I thought was essentially flat, it brought it to life in a really fucking eerie way".

There's no denying that. As the computer recites its speech, the effect is blackly comic and not a little horrifying. Computers do not, or at least not yet, have to worry about their saturated fat intake or being a more patient driver. Indeed, they don't have to worry about anything at all, as our capacity for emotion is precisely what is asupposed to separate us from them. The horror and humour lies in the computer's attempt to appropriate these emotions, although the facsimile's initially positive "thoughts" fall progressively asunder as the speech continues.

While the computer recites its litany, the sonic background is a terrifying picture of poignantly human acoustic music (strings and piano) being overwhelmed by samples, electronic distortions and ambient loops of computer sound (rather reminiscent of the classic score of *Forbidden Planet*, with its monsters of the id). Incidentally, one of the loops is from the 1974 film *Night Of The Condor*, which Thom had sampled from his hotel TV with his MiniDisc.

"Fitter Happier" forms the central axis in the album's meaning as well as its geography, which is why it's so powerful. The rest of the album rotates round it like a black hole and is similarly sucked into it. Therefore, if we are seeking a clue as to what the album's about, it's probably not a bad idea to see what's lying, smashed up and bent out of shape, at the bottom of it.

The track's electronic backdrop and indeed the computer itself are a fairly obvious concentration of the many electronic effects, digital loops and distortions that inhabit the rest of the album. The rubble of the acoustic music is a bit more difficult to pick apart.

The desperately melancholy, shakily played piano melody refers to a number of musical fragments that precede it on the album: the oscillating guitar jangles of "Airbag", the "We hope that you choke" vocal part of "Exit Music" and, most particularly, the opening guitar motif of "Let Down". The strings, meanwhile, take up the very chords that accompany "We hope that you choke", developing them to accompany this sad scene. In their instrumentation the strings are also reminiscent of "Airbag" and "Climbing Up The Walls".

The clue in all of this is, I think, in the references to "Let Down", whose emotional diffidence parallels both "Fitter Happier"'s melodic ambiguity and the vehement condemnation of "We hope that you choke".

"Fitter Happier" is, indeed, not about computers – it's about human beings. It's a warning of what happens when you don't take your own and other people's humanity seriously enough. This is as true of the wannabe aliens of "Lucky" or "Karma Police" as it is of the wannabe despots of "Paranoid Android" and "Electioneering". The noise in Thom Yorke's head is a siren of alarm.

08 ELECTIONEERING

If "Fitter Happier" is a warning, "Electioneering" is an urgent cry to man the barricades. "What can you say about the IMF, or politicians?" asked Thom Yorke rhetorically in *Mojo* in July 1997. "What can you say about people selling arms to

African countries, employing slave labour or whatever. You just write down 'Cattle prod and the IMF' and people who know, know. I can't express it any clearer than that, I don't know how to yet."

OK Computer can be roughly divided into two sections. Tracks 1-7 are a descent into the maelstrom of "Fitter Happier"; tracks 8-12 are a spirited although not entirely convincing attempt to restart life on the other side.

(Any mathematicians, masons and kabbalists may care to note that the divide comes 31'21" into an album of 53" 27" duration. Thus pretty close to the fabled golden section, a proportion one finds in all manner of artistic and natural phenomena).

As if newly galvanized by the awful vistas of "Fitter Happier", "Electioneering" is a spirited reassertion of messy, squalling humanity. The album bursts rudely back into life like the crying of a newborn baby.

After a slightly ominous start (linking to the previous track) somewhat reminiscent of The Doors and *Apocalypse Now*, Phil Selway's drum roll blows away the cobwebs of introspection and the band launch into a raw, jerky REM-influenced rocker that wouldn't have been out of place on *Pablo Honey*. It's the only time on the album apart from "Paranoid Android" when the band really gets to rock out. They sound angry, not least in the dissonant guitar solo, because they are angry. Radiohead have discovered politics, following in the footsteps of their one-time heroes and now peers, U2 and REM.

Before the band's involvement with War Child and their contribution of "Lucky" to the aid album *Help*, Radiohead's previous output was a remarkably politics-free zone. With this song and later the album's cover art, that was to be radically and permanently altered. The album cover, as you are doubtlessly aware, is an incredibly layered, cryptic lexicon crammed with more socio-political allusions than it's possible to list here (including shards of Esperanto, ritual hexes and the recipe for a Big Mac amongst other things) and there's a small internet industry dedicated to deciphering its mysteries.

Thom wrote the song after reading Will Hutton's *The State We're In* – a requiem for traditional left-right political polarisations – and modern-day Marxist Eric Hobsbawm's *The Age of Extremes* – a short history of the twentieth century. "I was completely fucking ignorant until I read those books" he was to enthuse to *Time Out*'s Peter Paphides in November 1997.

In "Electioneering", Radiohead have the unholy alliance of Big Politics and Big Money squarely in their sights. In a way unimaginable on their previous albums, Thom gives us a breathless reportage from the anti-globalisation front line, all the while undercut with petulant, complaining guitars: "riot shields, voodoo economics, cattle prods and the IMF, I trust I can rely on your vote." This journalistic approach was partly inspired by John Lennon's lyrics for "A Day In The Life" and is another example of *OK Computer*'s new lyrical mode of twinned observation and emotional reaction.

The main focus of the track's wrath seems to be the flagrant dishonesty of politicians, not least one T Blair, Esq, the current British Prime Minister, whose picture is widely assumed to be adorning the second page of the album booklet. A particularly amusing touch in the song is the *non sequitur* refrain: "When I go forwards you go backwards and somewere [sic] we will meet" which may refer to Mr Blair's "Third Way" rhetoric.

Simultaneously sung by two voices moving in totally opposite directions (counterpoint), they have absolutely no chance of ever meeting. Who said the musical joke died with Haydn?

09 CLIMBING UP THE WALLS

Once, claiming that his mission on Earth was to find "the ultimate atonal riff", Jonny Greenwood put out a message via the band's official newsletter asking anyone who had an unusual chord to write in. If he got any juicy ones back, it's a fair bet that he tried to slip them in the closing section of this song, the most frightening (in a horror movie sense) that the band had ever come up with.

The title says it all really. It's another of Radiohead's "psychological" specials, but this time the mind is as ugly and deranged as those of "Airbag" and "Subterranean Homesick Alien" are euphoric and airy.

Though revisiting the domestic setting of "Black Star", "Lurgee" and "Vegetable", the song does it in an incomparably darker and more terrifying manner. Like innocent suburban kids in a slasher film, Radiohead have stumbled across something utterly dreadful: "I am her face when she sleeps tonight/I am the pick in the ice/Do not cry out or hit the alarm/We are friends till we die." The "refrain" isn't much cheerier: "Either way you turn I'll be there/Open up your skull I'll be there/Climbing up the walls".

Deranged and increasingly unstable, as the song develops we seem to be trapped in the mind of a potential serial murderer. These are indeed monsters from the id. There is an interesting parallel to be drawn here with the progressively more dysfunctional computer of "Fitter Happier", as psychopaths are similarly unable to empathize or process emotions correctly. Thom's diction reaches new heights of menacing impressionism (with a corresponding lowering of intelligibility), but his voice is increasingly fractured and affected by delay and higher levels of distortion.

Thom has always been a great dramatic singer, straining to communicate every nuance of emotion, but this masterfully psychotic performance is a new high. The waves of additional vocals accentuate the effect of galloping multiple personality disorders as the song progresses.

The other band members have a ball, recycling their favourite soundtracks and mutating their guitars into all manner of strangeness. The harmonised "cricket/creepy noises", infinite tunnel guitar echoes and time-stretched/MiniDisc loops (including a first cousin of the one opening "Lucky") put us straight in to *Friday 13th*/David Lynch territory. The drum sound is brilliantly deadly as well, being captured mainly by ambient mikes that give it that dead-but-alive quality. The guitar solo sounds as if it's being played on one of *Forbidden Planet*'s theremins rather than anything with strings (something considerably developed on *Kid A*) and the growling bass synth adds the final touch of creeping John Carpenter-esque horror

As an extra bit of live location-specific weirdness, Jonny also "plays" a transistor radio during performances of the song in gigs, harking back to the glory days of John Cage and Stockhausen. As he told *Select* magazine in August 1997, "I'm tuning at random. I find two or three classical stations and two or three talking stations at the soundcheck and use them during the gig. I know what kind of music it is in advance – I don't want 'Size Of A Cow' to come out during the show." Quite.

Jonny told *Music Week* in May 1997 that he thought the track was, "Very string based, the white noise [at the end] is 16 violins. Frightening music. We didn't mean it to be like that: it just happened." Though the strings start off a little on the pedestrian side they perk up greatly after Thom's howl of nervous disintegration. In the final "white noise" section they're very effective, divided into Penderecki-style clusters, each instrument a quarter-note apart as if frozen in blood-drained terror. It's a sickening, enervated effect Penderecki made famous in his "Threnody". The combination of static "siren" strings with the equally rooted but quite differently-produced digital loops is both haunting and edgy, and would be exploited again on *Kid A*.

Recorded in Autumn 96 while the band were snugly ensconced at St Catherine's Court, who would have guessed that Jane Seymour's ballroom could sound so sinister?

10 NO SURPRISES

Radiohead have often not had the easiest of times in the studio but this track, in apparent sympathy with its music, was to prove astonishingly different - almost too much so, as Thom recalled to *Mojo* magazine.

" 'No Surprises' was the first thing we recorded," he said. "We'd bought all this gear, put it together and it was literally the first time everything was plugged in We pressed the button, the red light came on, and that was 'No Surprises'. The take on the album is exactly how we played it, bar a few small fixings. But we did six different versions of it afterwards, being anal. We went back to the first take in the end, because we'd discovered during recording that it's about catching the moment and fuck whether there's no mistakes or not."

In the overall "plan" of *OK Computer* as presented to us on the album, there seem to be two basic cross currents working; (broadly relating and connecting different songs by musical material, instrumentation, key etc). We've already touched on this in "Fitter Happier" but it's with the appearance of "No Surprises" that it finally becomes apparent.

Firstly there's a "positive stream", initially strong but slowly winding down: "Airbag" – "Subterranean Homesick Alien" – "Let Down" – "Electioneering" (a temporary revival) – "No Surprises" – "The Tourist", and a second "negative stream" which gets progressively stronger: "Paranoid Android" – "Exit Music" – "Karma Police/Fitter Happier" – "Climbing Up The Walls" – "Lucky". After the trauma of the previous three songs "No Surprises" is the point where we feel the "positive stream" to have been beaten (and hence discernible) and the mood of the album starts winding down.

I'm absolutely sure the band didn't write the songs to fit this scheme, but we do know that Thom Yorke spent two weeks rearranging the album's order on his MiniDisc, so he must have been reaching for something.

Though the songs are quite tightly related (far more so than on *The Bends*), the order is what provides the overall "story", the thing that turns a collection of songs into a cycle, a thing to be perceived as a single work. You need cohesion and direction to elevate things to that more powerful artistic level.

There seems to be no doubt in most people's minds that *OK Computer* is a genuine song cycle (i.e. a cohesive focused group of songs with an underlying theme) in the modern sense. Despite Roger Water's ambitions with *The Wall* the most successful example of course is Pink Floyd's *Dark Side Of The Moon* – it's not been in the charts for 30 years for no reason at all. Before that, *Sergeant Pepper* was possibly the last such work.

The song itself is as short and superficially simple as you might expect of a song called "No Surprises". It was written as a deliberate attempt to evoke the spirit (not the letter!) of The Beach Boys *Pet Sounds*, and with Ed's nostalgic guitar riff, Jonny's high-school glockenspiel and the infrequently used Radiohead tambourine given its second dust off in three songs, it succeeds pretty well so long as you don't read the lyric. It certainly sounds a long way from *Bitches Brew*.

Although the sections of the song initially seem to simply go round and round they are, like any good children's story, held together by some very clever, albeit diminutive twists and turns. Like the inside of a watch, it's fiddly to put things together on such a small scale, and difficult to see them working when they are. Nevertheless, have a listen for the relationship between verses that have the "No Surprises" tail and the ones that don't, the transformation of the verse's beginning into the "silence, silence" refrain and the lovely instrumental extension with its clever harmonic twist just before the end.

If we're musically still in childhood, lyrically we're definitely grappling with adulthood. Basically this is the angry young protagonist of "Vegetable" and perhaps "Black Star" settling down to the all-too-usual compromises of adulthood: "A heart that's full up like a land fill, a job that slowly kills you, bruises that won't heal/I'll take a quiet life, a handshake, some carbon monoxide, with no alarms and no surprises, silence/Such a pretty house, and such a pretty garden, no alarms and no surprises please."

It's a beautifully observed and very convincing lyric and Thom sings it with his usual aplomb. What I do find interesting is that someone who on the face of things wouldn't have to make those compromises somehow experiences them. Maybe being a rock star has its bad moments too. The contrast between the "adult" lyric and the music of the "childhood", which the singer is struggling to leave behind, make both seem more fragile and poignant.

Putting the song back into the context of the album once more, the congruency between the singer's place in the story of the song and the song's place in the story of the album, both subject to conflicting internal and external forces and both being forced to yield, is a spookily marvellous one.

11 LUCKY

In late August 1995, five months after the release of *The Bends*, Radiohead were approached by representatives of War Child, a charity organisation aiming to help the children of war-torn Bosnia. Under Brian Eno's aegis, the charity was putting together *Help!*, an all-star benefit album for which all the artists involved

"We did six different versions of it...being anal"

(Oasis, Blur, the Stone Roses, the Boo Radleys, Suede, Orbital, Massive Attack and Paul Weller) would record their contributions on the same day, September 4, 1995, so that the album could be in the stores a week afterwards. The band immediately agreed to take part and Jonny suggested that the band contribute "Lucky", a new song they'd recently been playing live to very good audience response.

At first Thom wasn't keen. He was still scarred by the *Bends* sessions and this song had been so easy to write and rehearse that he was suspicious. In the end he relented and on September 4 the band and Nigel Godrich entered the studio to record the track, finishing up just five hours later. The experience proved refreshingly different to the traumas of the *Bends* sessions and began the process of healing the band's recording wounds.

As Thom told *NME*, "There wasn't that sense of screaming and fighting and being on the phone to people for ages and spitting and swearing anymore...but that was never a help to anyone, I don't think... "Lucky" is a song of complete release. It just happened, writing and recording it, there was no time, no conscious effort." (*NME* December 9, 1995)

Later the same year Ed would cite to Mick St. Michael that the recording was his personal highlight of the year: not bad going considering Radiohead had also released *The Bends* to huge acclaim, had their first top 10 UK album, and performed in front of 130,000 people at Milton Keynes Bowl (on July 30) opening up for their teenage heroes REM.

Help! hit the shops on September 9, an amazing 5 days after recording. The album sold 71,000 copies on its first day of release and *Melody Maker* declared that "Lucky" gave "further weight to the theory that [Radiohead] are no longer capable of anything but brilliance." By the time the record was in the shops the band was already back in the US, opening for REM at the Miami Arena.

"Lucky" is an early manifestation of Thom's decision to try and write "happy songs" as per "Airbag". While not strictly a success by that definition, it's a lovely song nevertheless: bluesy, keening yet somehow hopeful.

Lyrically upbeat (or as upbeat as Radiohead tend to get), the song effectively plays "fantasy 70s rock bands" by persuading Jimmy Page to join a heartfelt but already unsettled Pink Floyd (crying Gilmour-like guitars, menacing "No Quarter" strumming and tremolos, Leslie Speaker-strangled backing singers, funeral mellotrons, etc) and then rather brilliantly juxtaposing the whole lot against the very latest in shimmering hi-tech "nails down the blackboard" guitar weirdness. It's a very disturbing effect, and shows the same love of contrast (real vs imagined, internal vs external etc) seen in many other places on this album, most pertinently in "Airbag", and on *The Bends*.

The eerie guitar noise was actually Thom Yorke's starting point for the song. It was like nothing we'd ever heard before" he told *Q*. It's apparently produced by "strumming the strings above the nut, where they wind off of the tuning pegs" and then, one assumes, shovelling it through some nifty digital cascades.

Thom sings like his life literally depends on it, hoping that the universe will hear and somehow respond: "I feel my luck could change, pull me out of the aircrash, pull me out of the lake, I'm your superhero." There's an obvious parallel to "Airbag" here in the hope of transportation disaster as a gateway to rebirth, but "Lucky"'s mood is more ambiguous. Quite whether it's the kind of thing to bring hope to the people of Sarajevo I'm not sure, but it's supremely effective.

It's this cross-pollination of lyrical and musical themes that gives *OK Computer* its coherency and "symphonic" quality: the feeling that we're examining the same basic ideas from a number of different but inherently related perspectives.

Two months after the release of *Help!* (November 1995) "Lucky" was released as a single to help promote the album and reached an unspectacular number 51 in the British singles charts. According to Jonny Greenwood, this previous release caused something of a quandary for the band when assembling the album's final track list. "We agonised over whether to leave it off, but we thought it was one of the best songs we've done. It just fits," he told *Music Week*.

12 THE TOURIST

After the emotional extremes of the trip – the visions, the euphoria and the psychedelics – comes the bone-crunching tiredness of the comedown: "They ask where the hell I'm going?/At one thousand feet per second/Hey man slow down, idiot slow down...."

Although completely different in musical style, the effect of "The Tourist" is very similar to "Goodnight" on the "White" album. Both are gorgeous, full of pathos and very hard to follow.

Thom wrote the lyric for "The Tourist" but Jonny wrote the music, the first time he had done so apart from some sections of "Paranoid Android". This is very much his track, and the guitar work is as central and imaginative as you would expect. Jonny, as is known, is a big fan of Pink Floyd, and the fact that the track is reminiscent of them is hardly surprising. But, as ever, it's very much Radiohead's own take on things.

There's a wonderful sense of ungraspable space about the track, as if the preceding songs were so far outside normal musical boundaries that now, on the other side, there is nothing to do but float. The track's very slow triple time makes it very difficult for the listener to get any sense of rhythm or orientation. Phil's brushed drums only add to the reverie, pulsing gently away as the song spins gently like a galaxy in the void. The bell seems to be the only definite point of focus.

Thom's vocal is so drawn out, slow and sustained that he seems to be less singing a song than providing a shifting vocal backdrop to the carelessly summing guitars: "It barks at no-one else but me like it's seen a ghost/I guess it's seen the sparks a-flowin', no-one else would know."

In the context of the song, the vocal, performed in a single take and sounding tired beyond any capability of expression, works perfectly but this was almost a happy accident. Like many songs on the album, the deceptively "wrecked" vocal was done in one take: "after that I'd start to think about it, and it would sound lame", Thom recalled to *Q*. "I really like the vocal on 'The Tourist' and I don't remember doing it. It was something we left on the shelf for months. When I listened to it again, I had obviously been told, 'Go out and sing a rough vocal so we can work on it.' There's no emotional involvement in it. I'm just, 'Yeah, Yeah, sing the song and walk off'. "

In the way that a concluding track ought to, "The Tourist" references many key musical elements from the rest of the album. The drums are like those of "Airbag", but are now drained of energy. The gently strumming and undulating guitars are now like tranquilized echoes of the many driving oscillating guitar figures throughout the album, gently falling when so many others had seemed to rise. Even the bell is like a faint echo of the kinetic high-school glockenspiel of "No Surprises".

The sweetly distorted "brown" Brian May guitar (of "Airbag" and "Paranoid Android") makes a last push between the first and second verses. After the second verse, the brighter Dave Gilmour-like guitar makes a second charge before being quietened by the masterly chord substitution that accompanies Thom's third vocal entry. Like a lightning conductor, it sucks all remaining energy away and the track spins down to rest.

The final bell becomes a wake-up call from the dreams and nightmares of the preceding 53' 27". *OK Computer* is quite a short album by modern standards – but feels like an age, in the most positive sense.

When the album was fully recorded and mixed, even Thom was happy in a characteristically oblique sort of way: "I was pretty convinced that we'd blown it, but I was kind of happy about that, because we'd got a real kick out of making the record," he told *Launch* magazine.

As events were to prove, he really needn't have worried.

scenes of *Meeting People Is Easy* is particularly revealing, as Nick Kent observed in *Mojo*. Thom, Jonny and Ed are sitting at a dinner table and Thom, not uncharacteristically, is unhappily berating his companions: "Jonny, last year we were the most hyped band. We were number one in all the polls. And it's all bollocks! Everything's changed and it's just a complete mind-fuck...I'm really, really worried. We've been running too long on bravado." Initially dragging the others somewhat reluctantly in his wake, Thom decided that the only meaningful course of action available was to draw a line under the band's previous output and completely re-imagine what Radiohead were all about in this post-*OK Computer* world.

When the band reassembled in Paris in January 1999 to begin recording, Thom had virtually nothing prepared. As he told Q's David Cavanagh: "New Year's Eve '98 was one of the lowest points in my life...I felt like I was going fucking crazy. Every time I picked up a guitar I just got the horrors. I would start writing a song, stop after 16 bars, hide it away in a drawer, look at it again, tear it up, destroy it...I was sinking down and down...I'd completely had it with melody. I just wanted rhythm. All melodies to me were pure embarrassment." Which was news to Ed O'Brien, who during rehearsals at the end of 1998 had envisaged the new album as consisting of pithy three-minute melodic guitar songs, and preferably Smiths-influenced ones at that. Gradually, over the next twelve months, as the band changed location from Paris to Copenhagen in March, to the Gloucestershire Mansion of Batsford Park in April and finally to their own newly-completed studio in

September, a way out of the creative impasse once again emerged. Following on from the *OK Computer* tour, Thom had been reacquainting himself with electronica, and in particular that of Sheffield's Warp label, whose entire back catalogue he'd reordered. Using this and other still more esoteric material as a starting point, he began to bring the band rhythms, sounds and textures around which their new music could coalesce. Even though they'd always been a jazz-influenced band, Radiohead would have to learn not only how to build upon this very new input, but relearn how to play together after fifteen very successful years.

For example, not every band member was to appear on each track. Even if they did, they might be in wholly unconventional roles. Everything was open for reassessment during this process, with absolutely nothing sacred. At one stage, the band was split into two separate composing/production units who were both forbidden to touch guitars or drums. Jonny, the band's ace lead guitarist, would mostly play ondes martenot, a pioneering electronic instrument from the 1920s, when he wasn't writing string arrangements or playing the recorder. If, as the *Rolling Stone* headline rather didactically put it, "In order to save themselves, Radiohead had to destroy rock'n'roll', what, the band themselves often wondered, was to replace it.

As Ed O Brien, who would hardly touch a guitar in 1999, later recalled to *Q*: "If you're going to make a different-sounding record, you have to change the methodology. And it's scary – everyone feels insecure. I'm a guitarist and suddenly it's like, 'Well there are no guitars on this track, or no drums'. Jonny, me, Coz and Phil had to get our heads round that. It was a test of the band, I think. Would we survive with our egos intact?"

"What we're going through at the moment – what we have to keep telling ourselves," Ed continued, "is that we're embarking on a new route...we couldn't have carried on the way it was before. There was absolutely no point. It's a cliché, but what we've done is split the band up and reform it with the same five members.You know, I think the one of the most important ethics of Radiohead is that we're not nostalgic. We never talk about school. We were all at school together, but we never look back. We never talk about what we've done in the past." If the band weren't nostalgic for past glories, you can be sure that their record company most certainly was. If they had been disappointed when they initially heard *OK Computer,* you can imagine what they thought on hearing *Kid A* for the first time. "Difficult" is the usual boardroom euphemism at these times for "commercially suicidal". Even worse, the band had decided that the album was to stand entirely on its own merits. There would be no singles, no videos, and relatively few interviews.

Faced with the challenge of marketing the seemingly unmarketable, Capitol, the band's US record company, through desperation did something very smart indeed. Realising the potential of the band's millions of incredibly dedicated and equally web-savvy fans, the company basically turned the marketing and promotion of this new album over to its audience.

To get them started, Capitol set up a special website, which not only included an instant "messaging buddy" as a bridge to unofficial sites (of which there are easily more than a thousand) but also steadily released information music and pictures, which fans could then easily and legally incorporate into their own sites. More radical still, three weeks in advance of *Kid A*'s official release in October 2000, band and record company alike encouraged fans to stream the album off the website and circulate free bootlegs across their own sites. The ensuing frenzy is widely believed to have been the final nail in Napster's already creaking coffin.

As groundbreaking as the music of *Kid A* undoubtedly was for a hitherto "front-line" rock act, the way its audience had first encountered it was without precedent, and yet as a marketing strategy could not have been more successful. Without radio airplay, hit singles or videos, *Kid A*, when released in October 2000, went straight to the top of the charts on both sides of the Atlantic. The band, their music, their methodology and their faith in their audience had been completely vindicated in both artistic and, still more remarkably, commercial terms.

Even bearing in mind the loyalty of the band's fan-base and, in the success of *OK Computer*, the matchless platform from which they were able to launch *Kid A*, the album could not realistically have done so well if it had not already been a great record. The reality that so many people already had the whole album lying on their hard drives without having to part with any hard-earned cash whatsoever in order to hear it, is probably the most eloquent proof of this fact of life.

UT: One-time Radiohead heroes and latterly peers

Although many in the UK regarded the album as "intentionally difficult", there were many plaudits too. The US gave Radiohead a Grammy award for Best Alternative Rock Album. The fans have been as steadfast as ever in their appreciation and, as previously noted, would vote *Kid A* 13th best album of all time in *Q*'s September 2001 15th anniversary poll, just below U2's *The Joshua Tree*: an almost unimaginable scenario to those listening to the very first downloads.

Lets hope that the lesson of *Kid A* and its success in some way leads record companies, shops and indeed some critics to adopt a more imaginative attitude to what a mass audience may, or more pertinently may not, find "difficult".

01 EVERYTHING IN ITS RIGHT PLACE

"Simple" and "difficult" are always dangerous concepts to throw around where music is concerned. Sometimes music that's labelled "difficult" genuinely is, but rather too often the word is just a bit of fear-driven bluster to disguise unfamiliarity with, or incomprehension of, what's actually happening. *Kid A* is fundamentally a quite straightforward, if extremely focused, album, "simpler" in some ways even than *Pablo Honey*.

The crucial difference between *Kid A* and the band's previous output is that this is primarily a music and sound-based rather than song-based record. In effect the album is a folio of ten miniature tone poems. This is not to say the songs aren't dramatic; they most certainly are. However, they're dramatic in the way of Beethoven's Ninth rather than, say, Lennon's "Working Class Hero". If further proof were needed, not only did Thom Yorke stipulate that the lyrics should not be printed on the album booklet, he also declined to explain them to the rest of the band, who were left to feel their way along like the rest of us.

Because of the sometimes scant framework in which the band had to work, there's a freshness and an almost childlike joy and sense of (re)discovery about the album. Stripped back to first principles as a band, they had no option but to trust their musical instincts, and be as honest as possible with their reactions and enthusiasms.

The very first track is a great example of this. A gorgeous, limpid but very groovy piece of minimalism, "Everything In Its Right Place" is based on a very simple idea but developed with real musical invention and playfulness. A title is always a good starting point if you're trying to put a song together, and so it's no surprise to see that the whole piece is basically a musical meditation on that phrase in the same way that "Stop Whispering" was on *Pablo Honey*. The "story" of the song is how each of its various musical aspects journeys to its own "right" place, wherever that might be. A tad abstract perhaps, but the total effect is mesmerizing; a multitude of different musical objects coming into and going out of focus, in and out of place, at their own rates, like twinkling stars.

Thom's jazzy digital electric piano chords at the opening encapsulate the piece in miniature. The three chords he plays are a jazzy "turnaround" of the kind used to finish a phrase or a piece. Starting on C, the song wants eventually to resolve on F, its tonal home: once it gets there, its journey is complete. Initially though, this progress is interrupted and the chords are forced to go back in on themselves, round and round, constantly frustrated - very similar, in fact, to what happens at the beginning of "Black Star". The journey the chords make in this piece to finally get back home to their "right place" and the "adventures" they have on the way, define much of its overall "story". As in other good questing tales, we meet some fascinating characters along the way. Thom's plaintive and impassioned floats in above bars of six and four beats, working against the metre until finally slotting into place on, fittingly, the word "place": "/6:...everything/4:/6:....in its right/4:PLACE'. This is, again, very reminiscent of the way changing bar lengths throw the emphasis around in *Pablo Honey*'s "You" and "Vegetable".

In many ways, on *Kid A* the band are basically picking up from just before their first album, and taking their musical predilections off in a different direction, as if

their subsequent career had never happened. This rhythmic cleverness and simplicity is paralleled in the melody's pitches. Though the chord progression is couched tensely in C, the melody starts blissfully "at home" in F, "Eve-ry-thing" which is what gives the vocal that tremendous lift. Gradually, though, it too is sucked down into C, hitting it on the word "place", rhythm and melody clicking together in the (temporarily) right place at exactly the same time.

The chord progression has the same major and minor ambiguity we've seen in many of the band's songs ('Creep', "You" etc) and, coupled with its relentlessness, has a strangely flamenco quality. Thom's bolero, perhaps. The melody then joins up with the chords in its own song-long journey from C to find peace back home in F

The quixotic verse lyrics are basically there for reasons of sound poetry. Supplying juicy sonic material in the same way we saw to a lesser extent in "Ripchord": "Yesterday I woke up sucking a lemon", "There are two colours in my head". Last, but by no means least, are the rhythmically but obviously not phonetically "in place" loops, cut-ups, and distortions of Thom's vocal, which are used to form background rhythms and textures. These blur the boundaries between "voice" and "instrument", making it a continuum, and subverting the usual idea of the relative place of each. These days we immediately think of Warp artists Autechre (in the cuttings) and The Aphex Twin (in their sound quality) when we hear these kind of processes, but it's worth recalling that they were pioneered in a very rudimentary way by Prince on his "When Doves Cry". Perhaps there was a point to the Headless Chickens" "Raspberry Beret" covers after all.

These different sonic characters are brought even closer together by the way in which they're processed and/or changed, (again shades of "Planet Telex") in similar-sounding but often technologically contrasting ways. The shifting, digital unreality of the piano, for example, works against the very tactile reversed, slowed-down, reverbed and filtered vocal "suckings" which are an old studio chestnut reminiscent of Delia Derbyshire's original work on the theme tune to cult UK sci-fi show *Doctor Who*. Again, it's all about what is or isn't "in place", when and how.

"Obscurity" and "difficulty", then, are hopefully revealed to be one musical idea, developed relatively simply, to form a self-contained, very cohesive and extremely beautiful world of sound. Brilliant as all this is, what finally makes the song is Thom's performance. It's so affecting, so wonderfully impassioned, you can hear how desperately he wants everything to be in its right place, however abstract that may be. It's this combination of passion, extreme musical sensitivity and focused invention that makes this track, and indeed much of the album, so extraordinary.

02 KID A

If the whole of the *Kid A* album is about musical fantasy and a return to first principles, then it's fitting that the title track should be named after a children's programme.

In contrast to the pithy processes of the previous track, "Kid A" is naive in the best possible sense. With far more regular rhythms and simple chord sequences to build on, the track is free to be about the sheer joy of making really cool noises. It's as if the "Kid A" of the title was a kind of musical Casper, leading band and listener alike into a musical wonderland.

As Ed O'Brien marvelled to *Q*, "You find yourself playing a Moog or operating machines that you've never used before. You're

Richard James: The Aphex Twin

literally like a kid: 'I don't know how this works, but God it makes a great noise!' It was so fantastic to realise that that's as valid as playing a really great riff on a guitar."

The sonic scene of this musical *Toy Story* is set straight away by the spacecraft landing sounds, train-set bells and digital toy pianos, all very reminiscent of the Aphex Twin and Skam Records band Boards Of Canada. Cute as they sound, these and the later time-stretches and "glitchatronic" noise are the result of some quite hardcore computer processing.

Ed to *Q* again: "Thom was encouraging and saying, 'Look _ this stuff is easy', and he's right. With all the technology and software available, you can take things and manipulate them in ways that you've never been able to do before. That's definitely something we're going to get more and more into: taking guitars and cutting them up, making sounds that have never been made. Everything is wide open with the technology now. The permutations are endless. Completely and utterly endless."

In contrast with the relative strangeness of these sounds, the drum samples are as simple as they are lovely, bashing away frenetically like the battery-powered drum playing rabbits in battery adverts. The bass plays along with them, the first "real" instrument we've so far heard on *Kid A*. The most arresting feature of the track, though, is obviously Thom's "vocal", the strange but seductive voice of a favourite electronic toy.

Though the lyrics, once again, seem to be used mainly for their sonic properties (not least because they're practically indecipherable without a lyric sheet), they pretty quickly take on an appropriately dark fairy tale hue: "I slip away, I slipped on a little white lie/We've got heads on sticks and you've got ventriloquists." It would seem that all is not quite as benign as it first appeared: "The rats and the children will follow me out of town....C'mon kids!" The vocal sounds disembodied because it literally is, time-stretched and then "vocodered" against Jonny's ondes martenot. The character, the "spirit" perhaps, of Thom's voice, has been electronically superimposed on the "artificial" pitches of the onde. It's a truly singular and expressive electronic voice.

As Thom told *The Wire*, the vocal processing used throughout the album allowed him, "to sing things I wouldn't normally sing. On "Kid A", the lyrics are absolutely brutal and horrible and I wouldn't be able to sing them straight. But talking them and having them vocodered... so that I wasn't even responsible for the melody...that was great, it felt like you're not answerable to this thing."

On the internet, Jonny talked about his obsession, "with the whole artifice of recording. I see it like this: a voice into a microphone onto a tape, onto a CD and through your speakers is all as illusory and as fake as any synthesiser – it doesn't put Thom in your front room. But one is perceived as "real", the other somehow "unreal". It's the same with guitars versus samplers. It was just freeing to discard the notion of acoustic sounds being truer."

03 THE NATIONAL ANTHEM

Like "Everything In Its Right Place", this very Beatles-esque track, which Thom credits with restoring his confidence after his bout of writer's block, is also about the nearness and farness of things.

In essence the track is a kind of sociological parable expressed by way of a "Music Of The Spheres" scenario. Around a central "ideal" core (of "D" ness), other notes are held more or less loosely as if on pieces of elastic. In art as in life, the notes on the periphery not only have more freedom but seem to be having a far more enjoyable time too. The result is what a national anthem (particularly that of England) would sound like if it accurately represented the real make-up of the nation and its people.

It's an ambitious scenario very redolent of 1960s veritée pieces like Stockhausen's "Telemusik" or the work of John Cage which so influenced The Beatles ("I Am The Walrus", or "A Day In The Life"), but then Radiohead have never been frightened of ambitious music. "We were very, very heavily into The Pixies," Ed O'Brien recalled to Mac Randall, "they were the most exciting band when we were at university. You always looked forward to a new album, and particularly when I heard (1989's) *Doolittle* for the first time I remember thinking, 'Jesus, this is going to take a couple of listens to get my head round it', and that's really important."

"The National Anthem" is similarly a piece that most people struggle to get their heads around. Perhaps the best way of listening to it is as a kind of giant jazz chord where all the usual jazz flavours of D (major) – colourations, extended notes, runs, licks, etc – gradually pile on top of each other (vertically), as opposed to being spread out in time (horizontally) as normal.

Holding the line, throughout the early stages of the piece at least, are Phil's satisfyingly clanky swamp-rock bass, spiralling downwards into D, and Thom's dreamily drugged-out voice. Add the Phil Selway shuffle, the background "radio" distortions and Jonny's gently meandering ondes echoing the voice, and we're heavily into "Tomorrow Never Knows"/"A Day In The Life" territory (we've seen the importance of drones and held notes in creating a psychedelic feeling many times in the band's previous music). Ian MacDonald's *Revolution In The Head*, a track-by-track analysis of the Beatles" music and recording methods, was apparently Thom's bedtime reading throughout the whole *Kid A/Amnesiac* recording process, and it shows. As well as various aspects of the music and production, the similar way in this track that jazz band (causing vivacious tonal mayhem!) and orchestra (an echo of a redundant past) are used for programmatic effect is striking.

As the band, and eventually all else, falls by the wayside, we're left to think Lennon-esque thoughts on the nature of society and the position of those "in charge": "Everyone around here…everyone has got the fear…holding on".

04 HOW TO DISAPPEAR COMPLETELY

This track has a very particular origin, being inspired by sudden feelings of sadness and disorientation that Thom Yorke experienced while on the stage of Dublin's RDS in the middle of playing to 38,000 people. The gig took place on June 21, 1997, just five days after the UK and Ireland release of *OK Computer*, and was their largest indoor audience thus far.

Once again this is based around a very simple idea, a piquant moment in time that suddenly and briefly comes into existence, only to be quickly lost, as the dying android Rutger Hauer says at the end of *Blade Runner*, like tears in rain. The question is, how to create this feeling of microcosm? How to communicate the frozen loneliness of being suddenly "spotlit" in the midst of a huge mass?

Frozen in time: Krzyszlof Penderecki

The sense of size, uneasiness and suspended time is created in large part by the strings, orchestrated by Jonny and recorded at Dorchester Abbey. The track opens with a seemingly never-ending and vaguely menacing string cluster (shades of Jonny's favourite, Penderecki once more) incorporating lots of beating, adjacent notes and the famous "Devil's Interval". It's made more disturbing still by being played with the bow near the bridge (*sul ponticello*) to give it that glassy, "unnatural" sound. This is a classic twentieth orchestral device which signifies "horror and weirdness".

To further heighten the sense of frozen time, the cluster itself is actually a very extended chord of F# which desperately wants to resolve onto B minor. The effect is that of an infinitely frozen penultimate chord, as if time has been stopped just before the very last chord of a symphony.

The band's entire performance takes place in this frozen space, somewhere in the crack between two climatic orchestral chords. It's rather like a famous episode of *Star Trek* where the crew encounters a life form that lives at a vastly accelerated speed. Kirk and co perceive their voices as a high-pitched buzz, while to the aliens the *Enterprise* crew were as good as frozen. This song is that buzz, constantly threatened by the impending wave of orchestral sound. Eventually the chord will be held back no longer and the band's brief song will be drowned, "disappearing completely": "In a little while, I'll be gone. The moment's already passed".

The contrasts in orchestration (the very immediate, folky voice/guitar versus its more classical strings) and key (whereas the stings are initially in B minor, the band are in its rather happier cousin D major) all add to the sense of the band being somehow disconnected from things, not quite solid. "That there, that's not me. I go where I please. I walk through walls. I float down the Liffey. I'm not here. This isn't happening."

The reference to the Liffey (the river that runs through Dublin) is interesting as there's more than a hint of U2 about the song. Similarities include Thom's mourning vocal, the high keening guitars that emerge from the haze every now and again, and the gently rocking, impermanent chord sequence similar to those of "Stop Whispering...", "Lurgee..." and "Sulk". The bass is fascinating, pacing round a related chord all of its own (A6+9) and studiously undermining Thom's harmonic efforts in the process. The occasional communal cadences (particularly those from G) are beautiful and full of pathos precisely because they're so obviously temporary.

The ambient Brian Eno

As the song progresses things wax before waning, the ah-ah voices shadow the guitars, and the strings and brass (sometimes strangely sampled) helpfully if somewhat mournfully join in to help the band along and accelerate their eventual, inevitable disappearance: "Strobe lights and blown speakers/Fireworks and hurricanes/I'm not here, this isn't happening/I'm not here, I'm not here."

05 TREEFINGERS

This song is as positive and life-affirming a mid-point of *Kid A* as "Fitter Happier" was a dreadful centrepiece for *OK Computer*. "Treefingers" is a gorgeous meditation on the slowed down, transposed sample of Ed's guitar that opens the piece. There's an obvious feel of Brian Eno's ambient work (eg "On Land") about the piece, as well as Can and the early Aphex Twin. However, the best analogy would be the Jimmy Smith Band playing a guitar solo on Mogadon, for the following reasons.

When a sound is slowed down this much, you can hear its overtones start to separate out and it begins to be perceived more as a chord than a sound. This gives it a "jazz organ cluster" quality. When this

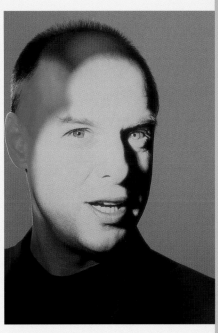

sound is then moved around, we hear it far more as a chord progression rather than a single line melody, particularly when it's done so slowly. In effect, what we have is a super slow, slightly strange-sounding bit of Jimmy Smith-style Hammond organ – an influence, remember, on the young Jonny Greenwood.

The clusters also recall the opening strings of the previous track (not least as we're back in F#, albeit major) and also the opening piano chords of "Everything In The Right Place". The title may refer to the smudging of notes as much the organic development, which is the other feature of the track.

As the cluster-chords change and go through their progression underneath, the guitars, electric pianos and other "sparkling" noises play through, and with, the less dramatically changing wash of overtones that each cluster sends up. This is a kind of "double-image" process, wherein the music exists on two levels at once: real and implied/imagined. It's exactly the same process that a be-bop sax player performs as he plays a solo, but here it happens in super slow, far more disjointed motion, and with bright sounds that themselves are loaded with overtones to further mess things up. All of which gives the music its shifting, incorporeal, ambient quality.

We're very much in the realm of the musical senses here, as the band responds intuitively to the shifting web of sound that they're presented with. You can hear in the many different guitar and piano gestures, and the static tangential samples, how subtly Radiohead respond to it.

The most obvious sonic parallels are the Vangelis of the early 70s, the *Blade Runner* soundtrack, and Pink Floyd circa *Meddle* (particularly that arching, soaring guitar). Lastly, as the piece progresses the bright scintillations become gradually more sustained and in tune with the underlying chords, growing closer together until they eventually meet. At that point, marked by a final electric piano toll, the piece is declared over.

06 OPTIMISTIC

Any fans who found the first half of *Kid A* intrinsically baffling must have been profoundly relieved by "Optimistic". At last, Radiohead playing a song as a band "live" in the studio! That said, it's a pretty dark and humid affair. Basically, this track is where the opening chords of "Planet Telex" meet the D-tuned open-stringed strumming of "Stop Whispering" and the tune of "Everything In Its Right Place" played by Joy Division or early Sonic Youth...in a swamp. For a bit of light relief, there's an intriguing coda where the riff is reprised by Talking Heads impersonating Chic (although still in a pretty sticky way, it must be said.) It's a pretty potent concoction, all in all, and with good reason.

"Optimistic" is *Kid A*'s "Electioneering". Not only does it similarly kick off the second half of the album after its mid-point hiatus, it also deals explicitly with the political issues that had become ever more important to the band in the years since *OK Computer*.

During the recording of *Kid A/Amnesiac*, three members of the band had read Naomi Klein's anti-corporate bestseller *No Logo*, and had been so affected by it that it was at one stage rumoured to be a potential title for *Kid A*. Ed O'Brien went so far as to urge fans to buy the book in one of his web diary entries.

"No Logo gave me one real hope" he told *Q*'s David Cavanagh. "It made me feel less alone. I must admit I'm deeply pessimistic about humanity, and she was writing everything that I was trying to make sense of in my head. It was very uplifting."

Naomi Klein: substance without signs

Yorke's take on things, as given to *The Wire*'s Simon Reynolds, was that spending three years in the UK after a long time touring abroad had been a big influence. He had been reading newspapers and noticing the discrepancy between mainstream, everyday pop culture and what was actually going on "out there" in the real world. On the anti-globalisation movement of which *No Logo* is the de facto bible, Thom said: "It's not really based on the old left/right politics, it's not really even an anti-capitalist thing...it's something far deeper than that: 'who do you serve?' It's a new form of dissent, a new politics."

These concerns certainly find their way into the lyrics of this raw and melancholic song, full of the routine violence and imagery all too familiar to anyone watching the TV with a shard of independent thought: "Dinosaurs roaming the earth/The big fish eat the little ones/This one drops a payload fodder for the animals, living on animal farm/vultures circlin" the dead, picking up every last crumb/Nervous messed-up marionette float around on a prison ship". There is hope, though, amidst all the gloom: "You can try the best you can, if you try the best you can, the best you can is good enough."

As Thom told David Cavanagh: "I can see the dinosaurs stepping over the mountains every time I sing that song...out of control monsters roaming the earth. All powerful, utterly invisible, wreaking destruction...faceless...nameless."

"It's all so part of the fabric of everything, even the artwork," he told *The Wire*, "I couldn't really say it directly so much but it's there – the feeling of being a spectator and not being able to take part."

While the UK sleeve of the album is quite abstract, consisting of solemn petrified icescapes, the US edition is more to the point. As well as featuring burning buildings, the crazed grinning bears that would find their way onto the sleeve of *Amnesiac*, and objects that look suspiciously like USAF stealth fighters on the back cover, it has a full page of statistics detailing "selected examples of ice melt around the world". After you've read a few of these: "Since 1850, the number of glaciers [in Glacier National Park, Rocky Mountains, United States] has dropped from 150 to fewer than 50. Remaining glaciers could disappear completely in 30 years", you start to wonder how Yorke sustains his optimism.

07 IN LIMBO

What do you do if you're stuck in a studio with your band mates, searching for a way out of your writer's block, but are so overwhelmed with ideas that you can't seem to focus on any one in particular? The answer, of course, is to put it all, or as much as you can humanly fit, into a song describing the experience. And that's just what Radiohead did with "In Limbo", another musical "documentary" in a similar vein to "How To Disappear Completely": "I'm on your side, nowhere to hide/Trap doors that open, I spiral down."

The original idea for "In Limbo" emerged during a soundcheck in New York in April 1998, and it was the first song the band attempted at the album's initial recording sessions in Paris. It's not surprising, then, that this track, more obviously than any other on *Kid A*, seems to follow on from the sound world of *OK Computer*.

At this point, the track was titled "Lost At Sea" and this was to become only too apt as the band rapidly seized up. "We soon became gridlocked", Phil Selway recalled to *Q*. "Paris was very much a case of us tripping ourselves up." Along with much else, "In Limbo" was put to one side and forgotten: "I'm lost at sea, don't bother me/I've lost my way."

As the days passed in Paris, ideas snowballed without resolution. "It was almost like a brain overload," Ed O'Brien said later to *Q*. "Human beings need a sense of order to handle things. If there are too many unfinished things, where do you focus? If you've got thirty or forty things started and you've made no decisions on any of them, it causes you to knee-jerk and panic at times. We had several crisis meetings".

How clever, and honest, then, for the band to find one way out of the mire by unearthing the song and using it as a vehicle for exorcising all of this in music. As Thom told *Mojo*'s Nick Kent: "I'm still proud of 'In Limbo' for the disorientating, floaty feel we managed to capture. It comes from this really peculiar place."

Acting on the time-honoured premise that "more is more", the band capture this feeling by taking lots of their favourite musical disorientation devices from the past and jamming them on top of each other in a chunky polyrhythmic layer cake. The nearest equivalent in the band's music is the mildly vexing minimalism of "Let Down", but this decidedly maximalist affair squeezes "Black Star", "You", "Airbag", "Kid A" and "Sulk" in there as well.

"I'm still proud of 'In Limbo' for the disorientating, floaty feel ...."

Radiohead are very fond of using aural illusions to disorientate the listener, and here they manage to get several working simultaneously right from the start. No wonder the track is confusing. The piece's very shaky foundation is the same "needle stuck in the groove" trick we saw at the start of "Black Star" (having a bar of six beats that's really a half, and a whole bar of four). This means the "start" of the four bar comes on the third actual beat, which is what produces the lolloping dub-reggae feel.

Cutting across the top of this in their own rhythm are the arpeggiated Andy Summers–style guitar figures. Running through chords which are quite far away harmonically (the "falling through fourths down a lift shaft" disorientation that underpins the chorus of "How Do You"), but played in a way that makes their notes sound very similar, it creates a classic "near but far" illusion that really brings the phrase "Trap doors that open, I spiral down" to life. The combination of the two gives the track its mutant "'Message In A Bottle' through the mincer" feel, and is presumably why Thom says the track reminds him of The Police.

"In Limbo" starts where *OK Computer* left off in more ways than one, and across the top of the guitars and drums is the jazzy *Bitches Brew* Fender Rhodes, complete with a cunningly shifting rhythmic pattern all of its own. The icing on the cake is Thom's initially deliberate, strangely crooning vocal, which has yet another "off beat in the verse, on beat in the chorus" rhythmic life of its own. This may be "difficult" rhythmic stuff in a Western/classical sense, but on the other hand people in Ghana, for instance, jam along to this kind of thing every day in the streets.

The band stir things up still further by contracting bar lengths, and playing with the relationship between harmony and melody, but suffice it to say it's all very cunning and admirably produces the claustrophobic, overwhelmed and panicked effect desired. Eventually, Thom can stand no more and starts howling in pain. The way the track dissolves into a babbling pitch-shifted cloud of conflicting vocals to leave nothing but mains hum is quite apposite, especially given the events of the period.

As Ed O'Brien wrote at the time in his internet diary: "There was very little played, but a lot of talk. The problem is that we are essentially in limbo".

08 IDIOTEQUE

After the preceding two "old-style" Radiohead tracks, "Idioteque" feels like a return to the laptop electronics of the "new" Radiohead. Such a distinction would be a mistake, though: there's only one "Radiohead" at work on *Kid A*. Quite often, as on with "Everything In Its Right Place" or "Kid A", the unfamiliarity of the electronics actually leads the band to travel musically back in time at the same time as it's going forward on orchestration terms. None of the "software" tracks are as musically complex as, for example, the more acoustic "The National Anthem", "How To Disappear Completely" or "In Limbo".

As Thom Yorke said to *The Wire*: "It's not about being a guitarist in a rock band, it's about having an instrument in front of you and you're really excited by it...It's like Jonny playing ondes martenot on...just about everything! We couldn't stop him! We had to beg him to play guitar on 'Morning Bell'."

The soundworld of "Idioteque" obviously owes a lot to the hard-core cut-ups of Autechre and child-like lyricism of The Aphex Twin, but there's also something of the "glitchatronic" work of even more avant garde acts like Oval and others on the Mille Plateau label. These guys often draw lines on CDs with pens so as to get them to deliberately skip and glitch between pre-prepared tracks, and it's a sound world also recently taken up on Björk's recent work.

This is not an easy world for a three guitar "rock'n'roll" group to take on board, and indeed it wasn't for Radiohead, but the fusion of the latest in digital technology with the dynamic of a skilled live band is a tremendously exciting one, and raises the electronica game to new heights. Having a drummer of Phil Selway's calibre on board seems to makes a huge difference for a start, and there's a musicality, plasticity and sheer funkiness to the rhythmic work in this track that raises it head and shoulders above other, similar tracks by rival bands.

There's obviously no guitar, bass, traditional drums or even keyboards in this very programmed track, and the question of what the five members of the band were actually to "do" in this kind of music, how they were going to be present in some way on what was after all billed as a Radiohead track, was a source of some worry for the band at first. The solution only came when, as Ed O'Brien explained it to *Q*, each band member had learnt the art of "how to be a participant in a song without actually playing a note".

Although the music of the song initially has much of the purity and playfulness of "Everything..." and "Kid A", lyrically it's a very different story, revisiting the political anxiety and sense of impending catastrophe of "Optimistic" and "How To Disappear Completely". Although childish concerns get a brief look in once again, it's under very different circumstances. There are the anxiously repeating "cut and paste" verses, telegraphing out their warnings: "Who's in a bunker, who's in a bunker, women and children first, and the children first and the children/Ice age coming, ice age coming, let me hear both sides, let me hear both sides, let me hear both." They contrast sharply with the naively complacent, more lyrical choruses: "Here I'm allowed,ev'rything all of the time."

If that glitching and editing wasn't arcane enough, Radiohead eventually follow the Yellow Brick Road of esoteric electronica (or should that be electronic esoterica) all the way to the rarefied Oz of academic computer music. As Thom prepared for *Kid A* he came across a lot of records via the internet, and that's surely where he came across the 1976 Odyssey label album First Recordings – Electronic Music Winners, The two composers sampled (whose publishers must have had heart attacks when the first post-*Kid A* royalty cheques came in) are Paul Lansky and Arthur Kreiger.

The extended "processed orchestra" sample at the track's end provides a nice counterpoint to the pure electronic and distorted rock sounds at the beginning of the song, and also ties in well with the orchestral instruments on the rest of the album, processing them in the same way as Thom's voice and the more "rock" instruments. Again, we're back in the realm of what's "real" and what's "imaginary".

The haunting "blowing into a bottle" tones that make up the opening "chord sequence" (shades of "Treefingers") are the sound of classic 70s academic electronica, which took six months to synthesise on the huge computers of the day what the DX7 could do instantly in the 80s, and your mobile phone can probably accomplish now. Naturally, this is because the huge corporations and the military-industrial complex have provided academic electronica with much of its funding, hardware and software in the first place for "research" purposes. The technology and many of the actual signal processing chips in an everyday PC soundcard, for example, started life processing radar in the nose cones of missiles or giant early warning systems: "Mobile's working, mobile's chirping/Take the money and run..."

Idioteques indeed.

09 MORNING BELL

Although probably the "simplest" song on *Kid A*, "Morning Bell" is in a way the most important as taken together with its twin on *Amnesiac* it gets to the heart of what *Kid A* (or maybe *Kid A* and *Amnesiac*) is (are) all about.

Before this track, various themes have run through *Kid A*: the possible "place" of things, their coming into existence and subsequent disappearance, transformation between various states of being – sometimes, on a physical and even political level, childhood and death, reality and fantasy, etc. Naturally, these things have also been present in Radiohead's previous work.

Arguably, however, *Kid A* (and *Amnesiac*) is ultimately about "potential": the multiple potentialities of a given thing, the different ways and directions in which it can be expressed. Not only does that theme underlie all the songs on this album; it's the very reason for its existence in the first place. *Kid A* is essentially a conscious effort to reappraise, rediscover and re-express "Radiohead" in a number of ways.

As we've previously seen, and will note further when we approach the band's live output, Radiohead's songs develop in a variiety of fashions over time. The unique thing about "Morning Bell" is that it's the only occasion in the band's output where we have two parallel "studio" versions of the same song. Its "potential" quality is thus given sharp relief for lacking definitive resolution.

The musical nitty-gritty of these related, but engagingly different, "readings" of the song is something we'll look at in the song's *Amnesiac* context. Suffice it to say for now that whereas the Kid-A version is couched in the jazzy bossa nova of "Blow Out" mutated via "Planet Telex", "Let Down" and "In Limbo"?, the *Amnesiac* version is the John Carpenter's *Halloween* of "Climbing Up The Walls" produced by the Phil Spector of "No Surprises". It's the same song, sure, but these are markedly different interpretations.

The root of this ambiguity probably lies in the song's subject matter, the "death" of a relationship and its impact on the couples' children, and hence the rhyming double meaning of its title. The "Morning Bell" of school is a piquant "Mourning" bell for the family: "The morning bell, the morning bell, light another candle/Release me, release me/Please".

This is the first time this "domestic relationship" area of the band's lyrics, which was such an important strand on previous albums, has been revisited. In true soap opera style, we pick up from the last "episode" of "No Surprises" or even "Black Star", where our lyrical protagonist was trying to reconcile himself to his routine domestic life. It would seem from "Morning Bell" that the relationship has since broken down completely. As with "Vegetable", there's also a whiff of domestic violence, but thankfully nothing on the scale of "Climbing Up The Walls": "You can keep the furniture, a bump on the head..."

The lyrics get darkly comedic, painting images of the hero having to look for the car amidst clothes and furniture on the lawn, before "sleep jacking" the fire drill: "Round and round and round..." I don't know what it means but it sounds as childishly spiteful and petulant as people often are in those situations.

Suddenly, though, the comedy ends: "Cut the kids in half. Cut the kids in half. Cut the kids in half. Dum dum dum... dum dum dum... dum dum dum... dum dum dum". This Solomon-esque command stabs home the reality of the situation, after which words appear to literally fail. Reality being too painful to deal with, it's much easier to retreat into childlike fantasy instead. Though the

"It's not about being a guitarist in a rock band, it's about having an instrument in front of you and you're really excited by it"

atmosphere of this version of the song is fairly dark, and Thom's vocal as strained as you might expect, there's also a quality of simplicity, even naïveté about: it's a kind of high-tech country-blues lament. Maybe it's the parents" way of coping: maybe it's the kids" only partial comprehension of what's happening.

There are similarities in the shape, evolution and vocal processing of this tracks' vocal/melody with those of "Kid A" and "How to Disappear Completely", both of which have a similar ambience of naïveté in the midst of darkness. This evolution – the majority of the words up front, followed by a simple coda at the end – is mirrored in the larger, two-part structure of the track itself, which has an extended "guitar" driven finale after the vocals have finished. This singular overall plan is another parallel with "Blow Out".

I use the inverted commas for the finale because although the band may indeed have begged Jonny to play guitar on this track, what he largely plays, apart from a brief interjection of "In Limbo" arpeggios, is a very striking hybrid of guitar and digital processing, sounding for all the world like the first cousin of the vocodered vocal on "Kid A". It's a further development of the digital "whammy" pedal-assisted jumps of "Just" and the guitar solo of "Climbing Up The Walls", and also strikingly parallels the "instrumental" transformations of Thom's voice in "Everything In Its Right Place".

The way that all these parallels and influences come together in "Morning Bell" make the song an indispensable vantage point from which to survey not just the rest of *Kid A* but also its place in the band's whole output so far. As if that wasn't enough, it also offers a glance into the future of *Amnesiac* and *I Might be Wrong*, making the track a major fulcrum in Radiohead's output.

10 MOTION PICTURE SOUNDTRACK

If *OK Computer*'s final track, "The Tourist", was an attempt to capture the feeling of the "White" album's "Goodnight" by other means, with "Motion Picture Soundtrack" Radiohead evidently decided to go for the jugular and beyond, creating a worthy climax for this most ambitious of albums. Thom has said that the track reminds him of the jaunty "Zip-A-Dee-Doo-Dah" featured in Disney's 1946 *Song of The South*, and the lush songs and soundtracks of the classic 40s/50s Disney musicals are the musical wellspring on which both tracks draw, in their very different ways.

The world of *Sleeping Beauty* was already a long way from the 1968 of the Vietnam War and the Paris situationist uprisings when the Beatles decided to pay a visit and, on the "White" album, the function of "Goodnight" is to graphically illustrate this. The affectionate, cloyingly pastiche of "golden age" media music ironically rounds off an entire album of the most utterly contemporary music which was then imaginable. By no coincidence at all, the album's "documentary" quality peaks in the very track preceding "Goodnight", the atonally fractured, psychedelically influenced, tape collage of "Revolution 9".

What Radiohead effectively do in "Motion Picture Soundtrack" is to refract "Goodnight" and its Disney ilk backwards through the cut-up lens of "Revolution 9". This isn't simply true on the later production/sampling level, either. As was the case as far back as "Planet Telex", the production of the

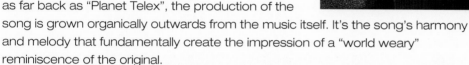

song is grown organically outwards from the music itself. It's the song's harmony and melody that fundamentally create the impression of a "world weary" reminiscence of the original.

This "beaten up" feeling is further cemented by Jonny's fantastically wheezy harmonium intro. The band surely must have found the instrument in a skip somewhere, or perhaps it's just the ghost of "Paranoid Android"'s missing organ coda. As Thom joins in for their first duet, the Tom Waits-style dinginess of the whole affair is so overwhelming you can practically smell it, like a drunk washed up at a Seamen's Mission. This is accentuated as the song's noir, even kitchen sink, lyrics spin a jaundiced narrative that Disney would have run a million miles from: "Red wine and sleeping pills help me get back to your arms/cheap sex and sad films help me get where I belong...I think you're crazy, maybe."

At the beginning of the second verse, a winter sun of frozen harp glissandos comes out to cast a brighter – albeit still chilly – light on things. Hearing this most sonically mobile of instruments pinned like a fizzing catherine wheel to a soundboard is a disturbing hint of what's to come. Thom Yorke's vocal sounds temporarily warmed, as if by a cup of hot soup, and the harp and harmonium are joined by a Hammond organ and a doleful, though benign, double bass that add to the Salvation Army feel.

On the second chorus the onde martenot joins in, ghostly but beautiful, and duets with Thom as he and the song rise to their lyrical, melodic and, it would seem metaphysical destiny in the clouds. That soup was obviously not quite warm enough: "I will see you in the next life". The earthly dystopia of so much of the band's early lyrics is resolved in the death/resurrection image of *OK Computer*, the ultimate transformation.

The onde martenot (left) with palm speaker (upper right)

Jonny's infatuatuation with the onde martenot, the instrument for which he largely forsook the guitar on *Kid A*, began as a fifteen year-old schoolboy when he heard first heard its siren song whooping and swooping its way through a performance of Olivier Messaien's cloyingly seductive Turangalîla symphony. This piece, incidentally, was memorably dismissed by Messaien's more austere ex-pupil Pierre Boulez as mere "brothel music".

"I spent years reading all these descriptions of them. I couldn't even find a photograph," he told *The Wire* at the time of *Amnesiac*'s release, "and then two years ago I finally got hold of one, and they're fantastic. The best way to describe it is a very accurate theremin that you have far more control of. The most famous use of the martenot is in the *Star Trek* theme, and it sounds like a woman singing. When it's played well, you can really emulate the voice. I get annoyed with electronic instruments because I reckon the martenot is a bit of a peak."

It's interesting to note that, even though the overall instrumental effect seems huge at this point, we really only have harp, organ, double bass and onde martenot present in the midst of some of "airy" white noise "tape" effects (reminiscent of "Nice Dream"). The lush Disney-style jazz chordal cadences, battered by the harmonium, signals the song's end and, as the harps spiral away into new-found harmonic areas and subsequent oblivion, the song finishes 3'17" after it began. Except, of course, that it doesn't.

"Motion Picture Soundtrack" is the oldest song on *Kid A*, with a history stretching back to the early 90s. A live version of the song "in progress" turned up several years ago on a Radiohead bootleg entitled *The Basement Tapes*, in which the song, far from stopping en route for the Pearly Gates, takes up the disturbing story on the other side. The further additional verses are reminiscent of "Nice Dreams"' tales of celestial partying and retributive electrocution: "Beautiful Angel, pulled apart/Limbless and helpless, I can't even recognise you". It was obviously felt, however, that a purely acoustic rendition didn't quite do the cinematic job, and so the song was shelved until it became possible to translate the spirit of this second half into purely musical terms.

A similar process occurred in the case of "How to Disappear Completely". The band part of this song is also present on *The Basement Tapes* (as "How to Disappear Completely And Never Be Found") but minus its crucial, "orchestra frozen in time" context. Again, the song was shelved until such time as it could be properly realized.

So it is that, after a silent interval of exactly one minute, "Motion Picture Soundtrack" begins again at 4'17". A faux glitch/tape edit heralds some introductory D's from the ondes, with the "orchestra" seeming to follow on as if tuning up (in their usual A) in preparation for the second movement/act (multiple nods here to the Beatles of *Sergeant Pepper* and "Revolution 9" perhaps). The term "orchestra" is relevant as this is no ordinary classical band: it's one heavily processed, cut and looped to the nth degree.

Right in the middle of tuning up, Radiohead are suddenly overwhelmed by the "angelic" choir, and amidst much backward digital "tape" reversal (the tambourines and cymbals are very apparent) orchestra and voices morph together into a timbrely amorphous but gloriously luminescent halo, centred on G major (the key of the song) but pulsing with varying flavours in a way reminiscent of "The National Anthem". Amidst what's left of the choir and orchestra there seems to be the remnants of other sounds from the album floating around, in particular a disembodied Fender Rhodes piano celestially telegraphing out.

It's as if all the instrumental and choral sounds of the Disney soundtracks and indeed "Goodnight" that had been absent from the first half of the song, had suddenly been thrown into an aural blender and tuned into a luscious sonic "smoothie", its now realized second half: "Beautiful Angel, pulled apart/Limbless and helpless, I can't even recognise you". Prefigured by Paul Lansky's sample, the orchestra has now fully achieved the transformation into pure electronic sound previously made by Thom's voice and the other more rock elements of the album's instrumental canvas. Remarkably, the most "real" of instruments have become equally imaginary.

Precisely 51 seconds after this second part of the track begins, it fades out at 5'08", leaving us in silence before disappearing from the monitor at 6'59". So, overall, that's the first part of 3'17", a gap of one minute, then 51 seconds of sound, then the silent sum of the two before closing. The numerical relationships between the last three sections are obvious, but what the numerology relating 3'17" and 1'51" is... I'm afraid I can't tell you!

Now, 1'51" in a track of 6'69" is a long time, and as there's already been one reprise, the listener assumes that there will be another. So we wait, and wait, and as we're waiting for the song to restart our brains are ticking over and trying to imagine what kind of music will come next. Shades of John Cage's famous 4'33" silent piano piece, perhaps?

With the now downloaded *Kid A* floating around in our consciousness, aural memories, particularly of the very last amorphous sound just heard, surface and superimpose like fragmented ice sheets. Each of us will have our "potential" ideas of where this virtual album should go next, and it's but a mental hop from there to the way it was distributed across the internet in the first place. At the point, for a while at least, the next development is down to the fans and the listeners.

" The most famous use of the martenot is in the Star Trek theme..."

AMNESIAC
2001

OK Computer gave Radiohead an enormous amount of artistic freedom. On *Kid A* they had decided to rebel. This rebellion was not just against music business practice, copyright law, global economics, and the expectations of what a successful rock'n' roll band ought to sound like. They principally rebelled against what Radiohead "ought" to sound like, a strategy met with a decidedly mixed reception in some quarters. As Jonny Greenwood commented acidly at the time of its release, "people basically want their hands held through twelve 'Mull of Kintyre's'."

After the album's release, the band continued their non-conformist stance by embarking on their No Logo tent tour, reaching the UK in September and October. Defiantly un-sponsored in a marketing brand-dominated age, they took a specially designed and acoustically optimised tent to as many interesting and non-standard places as possible. Ticket publicity was largely done by word-of-mouth across the internet, keeping the magic circle enclosing band and fans as tight as possible.

En route, the band naturally began to think about how to release the rest of the material from the *Kid A* sessions. At one stage, it had been mooted that *Kid A* be released as a double album and this might have been the best, if somewhat taxing, option. With *Kid A* already released as a single album, any follow-up would be open to being considered a selection of "out-takes" rather than a partner or continuation.

01 Packt Like Sardines In A Crushd Tin Box
02 Pyramid Song
03 Pull/Pulk Revolving Doors
04 You And Whose Army?
05 I Might Be Wrong
06 Knives Out
07 Morning Bell/Amnesiac
08 Dollars And Cents
09 Hunting Bears
10 Like Spinning Plates
11 Life In A Glasshouse

During this period, Colin Greenwood summed up the relationship between the two albums very well: "I'm not sure they are two records. We had that group of songs to make one record, and the other ones are left over. We had, say, 23 songs and we wanted to have around 47 minutes of music [for *Kid A*], so we chose the best combination out of that number and the rest are waiting on the bench, waiting to be picked for the next team line-up. *Amnesiac* is more conventional, perhaps, but also more dissonant. But it continues on from *Kid A*. It was all done in the same recording period. It is all a whole."

This next "squad" of songs was released as *Amnesiac* on June 4, 2001 and, as might be expected, hit the top of the charts on both sides of the Atlantic (UK No. 1, US No. 2), entering the UK chart at No 1.

Although more "conventional" in its greater use of guitars and song-based structures, *Amnesiac* also struck out in some intriguing and challenging new directions. Thom liked to frame the differing musical characters of the two albums in these terms: "I think the artwork is the best way of explaining it." He told *Mojo*, "The artwork to *Kid A* was all in the distance. The fires were all going on the other side of the hill. With *Amnesiac* you're actually in the forest while the fire's happening." It is, one might add, the difference between coolly surveying "new" influences and reconciling them with your existing music.

At the time of *Amnesiac*'s release, Thom had spoken of his boredom and frustration with his own voice and ways of singing before embarking on the *Kid A/Amnesiac* sessions, something perhaps symptomatic of his then attitude to the band's previous music as a whole: "It did my head in that whatever I did with my voice it had that particular set of associations," he told *The Wire* "And there were lots of similar bands coming out at the time, and that made it even worse. I couldn't stand the sound of me even more."

Thom described his way out of this cul-de-sac, *Kid A/Amnesiac*'s interfacing of voice and technology, as establishing "a grammar of noises", and this phrase is the key to understanding the underlying basis of, and relationship between, both albums. On *OK Computer* we saw how the band established a kind of "symphonic" cohesion between tracks by having a small number of central lyrical themes, musical fragments and production scenarios common to the whole. *Kid A/Amnesiac* works in a similar but more developed and abstract way.

The thematic elements of *Kid A/Amnesiac* are best thought of in terms of a "pack" of thematic cards, much larger than on *OK Computer* and less specifically centred on musical fragments. Instead, many more stylistic, instrumental and production ideas have been added to the existing "Radiohead" deck. There are more deeply expressed formative influences, as well as wholly novel ones.

Each track on *Kid A* and *Amnesiac* has its own particular "hand", a small selection drawn from the pack, and what we hear is a particular musical "reading" of it, tarot-style. The common factors are the band's musical sensibility and, in all but two cases, Thom's voice. The difference between the albums arises from the tracks' different thematic "hands", as well as the fact that on *Amnesiac* there's more room for the occasional wild card harking back to *OK Computer* and even more so *The Bends*.

Thom told *Mojo*'s Nick Kent, after the album's release, that the band, "had this whole thing about *Amnesiac* being like getting into someone's attic, opening a chest and finding their notes from a journey that they've been on [the reason for the album's book packaging]. There's a story but no literal plot, so you have to keep picking out fragments. You know something really important has happened to this person that's ended up completely changing them' but you're never told exactly what it is."

What could be more important to a musician than his musical life-story? The reason for choosing the new album's title, Thom explained to *The Big Issue* was that "it's about... it's about... the things you forget. And remembering."

01 PACKT LIKE SARDINES IN A CRUSHD TIN BOX

"Kraftwerk go to a field trip to India with George Harrison", is probably the best, if unlikely, way of describing this effervescent opener to *KidA/Amnesiac*'s "second eleven". There seems to be a large dose of subtle comedy in the track too. Thom and the chaps are obviously peeved at someone, but it's difficult to know precisely who.

The atmosphere is established straight away by a "field recording" of the gently modulated Hare Krishna "water drum". No sooner have we placed ourselves by the side of the Ganges than a distinctive popping kick and white-noise snare lets us know that the men from Köln have arrived with a bus-full of their Computer World technology in tow. What's very cool (and not a little funny) is the way Radiohead integrate these most unlikely of musical bedfellows. As the full gamut

of Kraftwerk's distinctive sound palette is successively and lovingly unleashed (distorted beeps, noise, lonely electric piano, ring-modulated digital "bells", skipping kicks, etc) it's put in a context that makes it seem absolutely at home with the Indian rhythms, atmospheres and drones that gradually form the track's overall context – not least the climatic Bombay street scene cacophony.

Particularly heroic duty in the drone department is done by the "chanting" processed vocals, the strings, and Jonny Greenwood's heroically evocative and often "reversed" guitar (owing more than a little to *Revolver*'s "Love You To" in particular). Over the top of all this Thom Yorke, ever the devotional singer of dystopia, turns George's quest for enlightenment ruefully on its head: "After years of waiting, nothing came/As your life flashed before your eyes/You realize...you're looking, looking in the wrong place/I'm a reasonable man/Get off, get off, get off my case". Getting on Thom's case, amongst other things, is a strong element of de-personalization and unthinking mechanization in the theme and lyrics of the song.

As Thom told *The Wire*, "We used autotuner (a vocal processing programme made most famous by Cher on "Believe") on *Amnesiac* twice. On "Packt Like Sardines In A Crushd Tin Box", I wasn't particularly out of tune, but if you really turn the autotuner so it's dead in pitch, it makes it go slightly…" (At this point, Thom made a nasal de-personalized sound). It sounds like a less pronounced version of the effected vocal on *Kid A*'s "Morning Bell'.

On the other hand, the echoing sequencer "jams" with their random, interchangeable notes are a wry steal from Kraftwerk's "Numbers". Like much of the *Computer World* album the track is a somewhat chilling evocation of man's reduction to the anonymous digital data of the machine world (as previously defined on *OK Computer*'s "Fitter Happier").

The song's lyrics, vocal de-personalization, title and warnings of machine dehumanisation, all set in a quasi-religious Indian context, would seem to point to a suspicion of unthinking (Western rock-star?) off-the-peg enlightenment. This impression is reinforced when, towards the end of the song, the voices chanting along with Thom seem to degrade into something distinctly less human. Is this the "market" noises of sacred cows and bleating sheep, perhaps?

Cher can't "believe" what Radiohead have done with her autotune

02 PYRAMID SONG

In its very short public existence, "Pyramid Song" has changed title no less than three times. First heard at the 1999 Tibetan Freedom Concert, with Thom on the piano, the track later adopted the title "Nothing To Fear". This was changed to "Egyptian Song" at London's Meltdown festival in 2000, before finally emerging on *Amnesiac* the following year as "Pyramid Song".

Fear and pyramids are quite a singular combination as anyone – not least Mark Twain – who has braved the swarms of over-eager Giza plateau tourist hustlers will tell you. The origin of this image is, of course, the biblical plight of Moses and the Israelites in Egypt, and the even earlier biblical troubles "by the waters of Babylon". Adopted several millennia later as a symbol of black suffering in America, Moses' travails eventually found their way into "Freedom" a haunting political "spiritual" by Charles Mingus, which is where it enters the Radiohead story.

"'Pyramid Song' is me being totally obsessed with…'Freedom'," Thom told *Mojo*'s Nick Kent, "and I was just trying to duplicate that really. Our first version of 'Pyramid Song' even had the claps that you hear on 'Freedom'. Unfortunately, our claps sounded really naff, so I quickly erased them."

Thom has cast "Pyramid Song" in a similarly spiritual style but his take on the blues seems, at first, to be geographically askance. The tracks flamenco chords are similar to those of *Kid-A*'s "Everything In Its Right Place" for the very good reason that they "were both written in the same week – the week I bought a piano,"

Thom told *Mojo*. "The chords I'm playing involve lots of black notes. You think you're being really clever playing them but they're really simple. For 'Everything In Its Right Place' I programmed my piano playing into a laptop, but 'Pyramid' sounded better untreated."

The particular way the opening chords rise and fall (F#, G, A), their initial semitone step and the fact they're all major chords goes a long way to creating this "deep song of the flamenco" rather than a black/African feel. Naturally there are other harmonic wrinkles, but the really important thing about the song is Thom's vocal. It's an elemental performance, and one of the album's highlights.

The song's spiritual feel is carried through into its lyrics, which are strangely reminiscent of the famous Negro spiritual "Swing Low, Sweet Chariot". Thus instead of "I look o'er Jordan" etc we have: "I jumped in the river, what did I see?/Black-eyed angels swam with me/A moon full of stars and astral cars/All my past and futures/And we all went to heaven in a little row boat/There was nothing to fear and nothing to doubt".

The spine-tingling, wonderfully responsive string /onde arrangement is another album highlight. The way Thom's cooings are picked up (using false harmonics on a single string) to give that very unearthly swooping Aeolian harp sound is scrumptious. As the track evolves, blooming ever richer and more full-bodied, straining ever more urgently against the pulsing bass and drums tethering it down, one can't help being moved by the guts and passion in the same way as by more traditional flamenco.

The eerily processed, fractured "pipes" that look on so mournfully throughout this "deep song" make me wonder if any of this bondage is of a more contemporary, South American kind. After all, they have pyramids too.

In interviews after *Kid A*'s release, the band tried to sooth jangled industry and critical nerves by making much of the forthcoming "back to the guitar" normality of *Amnesiac*. As Thom said in an interview at the time; "With the next one [*Amnesiac*]

we are definitely having singles, videos, glossy magazine celebrity photo shoots, children's television appearances, film premiere appearances, dance routines and many interesting interviews about my tortured existence."

So it was that, three and a half years after the release of the band's last single, "No Surprises", and two weeks before *Amnesiac* itself, "Pyramid Song" was released as the albums first single on May 21, 2001. Despite being rather less commercial, it almost emulated its distant predecessor's high UK chart position, falling only one place short at a very credible number five.

03 PULL/PULK REVOLVING DOORS

Radiohead are fairly settled chaps at heart and, despite the periods of angst that seem to envelope the decision-making process, have evolved a remarkably consistent template for what a Radiohead album's track order should sound like. As such, the degree to which *Amnesiac* corresponds to its predecessors might throw some light on whether this second team really is a Radiohead album or, as darker voices initially suggested, a collection of *Kid A*'s outtakes. In brief, the archetypal Radiohead album (so far) follows the following pattern

Track 1: Effervescent opener:
"You", "Planet Telex", "Airbag", "Everything In Its Right Place".

Track 2: Weighty and thematic, often the title track:
"Creep", "The Bends", "Paranoid Android", "Kid A".

Track 3: Musing euphoric fantasy:
"How Do You?", "High And Dry", "Subterranean Homesick Alien", "The National Anthem".

Track 4: Eerie examination:
"Fake Plastic Trees", "Exit Music", "How To Disappear Completely".

Track 5: Not so light relief (if tracks allow):
"Thinking About You", "Bones", "Let Down"/"Karma Police".

Track 6: Mid point hiatus:
"Stop Whispering", "[Nice Dream]", "Fitter Happier", "Treefingers".

Track 7: Upbeat second half restart song with a message:
"Anyone Can Play Guitar"/"Ripcord", "Just", "Electioneering", "Optimistic".

Track 8: Creepy spanner in the works:
"Vegetable", "My Iron Lung"/"Climbing Up The Walls", "In Limbo".

Track 9: Wistful last hurrah:
"Prove Yourself", "Bullet Proof", "Idioteque".

Track 10: Domestic Resignation:
"I Can't"/"Black Star", "No Surprises", "Morning Bell".

Track 11: Sulky Song:
"Lurgee", "Sulk", "Lucky", "Motion Picture Soundtrack" (1st half).

Track 12: Expansive closer
"Blow Out", "Street Spirit (Fade Out)", "The Tourist", "Motion Picture Soundtrack" (2nd half).

So far so good, then. "Packt Like Sardines In A Crushd Tin Box" and "Pyramid Song" fit into this framework neatly, and "Pull/Pulk Revolving Doors" certainly fits alongside the meditative fantasy of "Subterranean Homesick Alien" and "The National Anthem".

The song's lyrics do indeed concern doors and their life-changing powers: "There are barn doors/And there are revolving doors/There are doors that let you in/And out/But never open/But they are trapdoors/That you can't come back from". As the lyrics are barely intelligible, though, the most important aspect of them is probably their concern with transformation and altered states.

Hip-hop descendent D.J. Shadow

That's what the track is musically about, at any rate, with all manner of processing having been applied to the sounds that form its raw material. Even the breakbeat drum pattern appears in a double image, the kind of slap-back "the same record on twin decks" effect so beloved of early hip-hop DJs and their musical descendants. The whole atmosphere of the track puts one in the mind of a drugged-out version of early Public Enemy.

The pounding, distorted drumbeat is by far the most "sober" aspect of the track and after the initial "mixer scratches" (quick fade in and outs) one half expects the young Chuck D to blaze in, bringing the noise or at least lambasting the Radiohead lads for their tea-drinking limey wussiness. But it doesn't happen like that, and almost instantly, all manner of obsessive and heavily transformed psychedelic weirdness takes hold (Hammond organ turned into sitar, for example) before the pipes of "Pyramid Song" eventually round things off at the end with an appropriate reprise of the "needle in the groove" trick.

The Indian-tinged electronic trance effect is obviously very evocative of "Packt Like Sardines In A Crushd Tin Box" and several other previous tracks on *Kid A/Amnesiac*, but here it occurs in a very much more concentrated and literally compressed form.

Yet the most striking aspect of the track is, undoubtedly, Thom's matter of fact anti-rap. This amazing effect was also achieved with the aid of the same autotuner computer programme that was used on "Packt…". "There's this trick you can do", Thom told *The Wire*, "where you give the machine a key and then you just talk into it. It desperately tries to search for the music in your speech, and produces notes at random. If you've assigned it a key, you've got music."

04 YOU AND WHOSE ARMY?

Though the casual listener might be unaware of it, this gorgeous piece of understated agit-prop is probably Radiohead's most politically pointed song to date. The target of its smoky venom is long time Radiohead villain, UK Prime Minister Tony Blair, together with, in the band's view, his equally craven cohorts.

Originally, Thom told *Mojo*'s Nick Kent, the song "was about the voices in my

head that were driving me round the bend – to be honest… And then, once I came up with that 'You and Whose Army' phrase, I was able to stick other ideas on there, and Blair emerged as the song's real subject matter. The song's ultimately about someone who is elected into power by people, and who then blatantly betrays them, just like Blair did. I call him 'a fool' because a fool is just someone who plays to the court; he's a court jester, but that's basically the same with most presidents these days."

Following in the tradition of "Motion Picture Soundtrack", "Karma Police" and, to a certain extent, "Packt Like Sardines In A Crushd Tin Box", the song evokes the music of several decades ago to make an ironic point. In this case, the Second World War era vocalizing of groups like The Ink Spots is pressed into service to frame and underline the third-wave conflict between Big Money and the anti-globalisation/No Logo movement. The song's initially languid atmosphere contrasts to great effect with its petulant battle lines lyric: "Come on if you think you can take us on: You and whose army?/You and your cronies". It's a touch of musical escapism, for sure, but to a serious purpose. As Thom told *The*

Wire: "The reason people are so into escaping is that there's a fucking lot to escape from....".

The band went to great lengths to recreate the 40s feel, as Thom recalls; "We hired all of these old ribbon microphones, but it didn't work because you need all the other gear, like the old tape recorders. So what we ended up using is an egg box. And because it's on the vocal mike, and the whole band's playing at the same time, everything on the track goes through the egg box."

Given the atmosphere of the track, it should come as no surprise that another piece of antique recording technology, Jonny's now ubiquitous ondes martenot, is working its own brand of ghostly magic in the capacity of celestial backing singer, alongside the band's more flesh and blood versions. As in the case of "Karma Police", Radiohead don't just nail the musical style and leave it at that. This is no static pastiche, and the whole point of establishing the 40s style is to bend and change it.

Bouncing Bud Powell

The bending starts with the second chorus and the appearance of the very singular halo of "melting" reverberation round Thom's voice. Also heard on *Kid A*'s "The National Anthem", this effect is created by playing Thom's vocal though the onde's palm speaker. This is basically a speaker with a harp strung over the top of it, giving out sympathetic vibrations like a sitar.

While this is happening, the underlying chord sequence, reminscent of pioneering jazz pianist Bud Powell whose music Thom played thoughout the entire *Kid A* and *Amnesiac* sessions, is also morphing, becoming less jazzy and more Beatlesque. This is something pushed much further still via one of Thom's beloved major/minor chord twists when the band assemble for the song's gripping climax: "You forget so easily/We ride tonight/Ghost horses". The mood of the song... has now been swung round completely from irony to evocation to rallying call. It's a wonderful moment. If the anti-globalisation movement could summon up strategy, invention and energy on this level, Blair and co would have to make very hasty plans for early retirement.

As regards our archetypal album template, "You And Whose Army", undoubtedly, qualifies as a worthy successor to "Fake Plastic Trees", " Exit Music" and "How To Disappear Completely".

05 I MIGHT BE WRONG

One of the most constant and important factors in Thom Yorke's personal life is his relationship with long-time partner Rachel Owen. The two met while still students at Exeter, and Thom has spoken on many occasions of the myriad positive effects she has had on his life. These very personal feelings inform the writing of "I Might Be Wrong".

"It's a document of a complete crisis point, basically", Thom told *Mojo*. "I live on a beach, and one night I went on my own and looked back at the house and even though I knew there was nobody there, I could see a figure walking about inside. Then I went back in to the house and recorded that track with this presence still there..."

"The song really comes as much from what Rachel was saying to me, like she does all the time: 'Be proud of what you've done. Don't look back and just carry on like nothing's happened. Just let the bad stuff go'. When someone's constantly trying to help you out and you're trying to express something really awful, you're desperately trying to sort yourself out and you can't , you just can't. And then one day you finally hear them – you finally understand after months and months of fucking torment. That's what this song is about."

The lyrics are remarkable for the way they not only frame but also poetically enhance these thoughts: "I might be wrong/I could have sworn/I saw a light coming on/I used to think/There is no future left at all/I used to think/What would I do?/If I did not have you/It's nothing at all".

The contrasting effects of these "presences", good and bad, in Thom's life find musical expression in a number of ways. Foremost among them is the contrast between the soothing, gently reflective vocal and the restive music beneath. The latter is itself full of oppositional elements; the carelessly bouncing drone of the Delta blues guitar working against the skipping precision of the two-step drums, while under and around them bubble polyrhythmic bass, acid synth and echoing scratches. That this is further counterpointed by shaped white noise (the sound of breaking waves perhaps) is particularly neat.

Publicly debuted in Italy on June 19, 2000, the song's title is rather appropriate as regards to our Radiohead album "template" as it's the first partial departure on the album from it. In fact, it rather economically combines the roles of upbeat "relief" and dreamy mid-point hiatus. If we wanted to be pedantic, we might try and "force" the guitar driven coda into the latter role, but it doesn't quite cut it. "Skewed combination" probably best describes it.

The deeper and more personal something is, the more difficult it can be to express, and this may be alluded to in the Catachresis College origin of the album's limited edition "library book" format. "Catachresis", as derived from the Greek, is the term for the incorrect use of words in either meaning or context. Such, we must acknowledge, are the expressive benefits of a good education.

06 KNIVES OUT

The second half of *Kid A/Amnesiac*'s second eleven is opened by the propulsive but still dreamy "Knives Out". Originally premiered in acoustic form on the band's first surprise webcast on December 9, 1999, it's since been introduced live as "a song about cannibalism". We appear to be on safe ground with that one: "So knives out/Cook him up/Squash his head/Put him in the pot."

While its combination of breeziness, Guignol humour and an accusatory tone have other relatives in the Radiohead canon (e.g. "Karma Police"), the most direct lyrical and musical ancestor of this piece is the quasi-baroque "rain down" section of "Paranoid Android". In fact, this is by far the most traditional, "guitar driven" song on either *Kid A* or *Amnesiac*, and wouldn't have been that out of place amongst the last few songs of *Pablo Honey* or *The Bends*.

What ties the song into *Amnesiac*, though, is the serpentine intermeshing of the guitar parts, delicately enfolding some quite thorny dissonances thrown up by the gently head-spinning, baroque chord sequences and their associated key changes. Putting the listener in harmonic free-fall, they have a similar disorientating effect to the more brutal polyrhythms of "In Limbo". Another subtle post-Bends element is the lurking hint of electronic weirdness in the shape of the frozen vocal halos once again around Thom's voice.

The elegant sweep of the melody and the song's overall harmonic flow has a definite air of jazzed-up classical/Spanish guitar, which also ties up with "Pyramid Song"'s flamenco influences. Sounding like one of the *Lord Of The Flies*' more degenerate subjects, Thom's distracted but compelling schoolboy vocal is conspiratorially cocooned by the band, who dive in to surf the song's dramatic cadences together and set the lyrical madness off to great effect: "So knives out, catch the mouse/Don't look down, shove it in your mouth."

Apart from anything else the song nearly managed to consume the band itself, taking no less than 373 days and 313 hours to complete. As Thom, not surprisingly, told *Mojo*: "For the longest time, I really, really hated that song." "Knives Out" was the second single to be released off *Amnesiac* (on August 6, 2001) and reached number 13 in the UK singles chart.

07 MORNING BELL/AMNESIAC

If the "Morning Bell" of *Kid A* is touched by a bluesy spirit of lamentation, this nightmarish remembering of the same song is haunted by the twin ghosts of the Beatles and John Carpenter's *Halloween*. Another succulent slice of musical black comedy, "Morning Bell/Amnesiac", the album's "title" song is the Lennon-esque "Karma Police" by way of a "Climbing Up The Walls" slasher movie. It's the "Mourning Bell" of childhood taken "literally" in a tale of the very unexpected.

If further proof of this is required, other than the deranged fairground organs, carousel glockenspiels and queasily distorted atmosphere borrowed from the soundtracks of so many early 80s films, direct your attention to the music underscoring the cheerily demented climax of the song: "Cut the kids in half, cut the kids in half, cut the kids in half, cut the kids in half". It's pure Carpenter, all chromatically crawling digital pianos and obscenely flutey onde/analogue synths. Radiohead are acknowledged soundtrack buffs, and Carpenter is perhaps the most underrated soundtrack composer working today, defining the slasher movie score as surely as John Barry did the 60s spy soundtrack.

It's amazing how this new musical spin transforms the song. In the *Kid A* version the above line is the song's heart-wrenching climax; here it's the comically horrific denouncement of what we've suspected from the songs start

Similarly in the *Kid A* version, the line " Where'd you park the car…" is the prelude for some piquant comedy. Here, with that dissonant low synth suddenly lurking around in the fairground car-lot, it's setting us up for imminent blood letting, aided and abetted by the *Friday 13th* wordless chorus. As for the "sleepy-jacked" fire drill, happily spinning "round and round and round…" it's probably best not to think too deeply about it.

The reason why these two equally idiomatic readings of the song are possible is that the song's rolling, chromatically changing two chord pattern, which so elegantly mimics the shifting tone colour of the title's tolling bell, is as potentially evocative of Antonio Carlos Jobim's Bossa Nova as it is of the Beatles as it is of Carpenter. How it's heard depends very much on which musical stage it's playing on.

"For the longest time, I really, really hated that song…"

Firstly, the scenery. The instruments of *Kid-A*'s version are as skew jazzy as these are warped fairground. Secondly, the costumes. In the "smoother" version of the song on *Kid A* the two chords are both jazzy flavours of A. In the chunkier, scarier version of *Amnesia*, the difference between the chords is made stronger and more jarring by condensing the two flavours into two very discrete Beatle-esque chords, a broadly similar motion to that occuring in *Kid A*'s "How To Disappear Completely".

Finally, choreography. There's a real rhythmic difference between the two tracks. In the version on *Kid A*, each changing chord "toll" is expressed as a bar of five skipping beats, the irregular number of beats, quick tempo and shuffling groove helping to float things along and mask the "tolling" quality. In this version, each harmonic toll is transformed into a two clanging Lennon-esque crotchets (think "Imagine" or "Free As A Bird") or half of a much slower 4/4 bar. If you do the math, you'll see the chords last for about the same time, even though the effect is utterly different. Here, the plodding tempo and funereal articulation are juxtaposed against the jangling, gaudy brightness of the fairground to menacingly humorous effect.

If we refer back to our archetypal Radiohead album, we can see that this changed emphasis from domestic trauma to horror movie has a corresponding effect on the tracks programmability. The song thus moves further up the tracklisting from *Kid A*'s archetypal track 10: "domestic resignation" to *Amnesiac*'s more archetypal track 8: "creepy spanner in the works". After the blurring of the previous two tracks, there's no doubt the function of this one.

There's a weightier aspect to this version, too, as might be expected given the album's "title" song status. Whereas in previous decades there would, for reasons of cost and convenience, be only one definitive "studio" version of a song, as opposed to any live or remixed reinterpretation, the advent of cheap recording technology has revolutionized things completely. Here on the same "album" we have two equally valid readings of the same song, and there may have been others.

Release these into the distribution maelstrom of the internet and its hundreds of thousands of potent home studio set-ups, and it's likely that in the very near future there will be hundreds if not thousands of artistically if not legally valid "readings" of the same song; those of the originating artist, and further versions added to or transformed by concentric circles of remixers and co-composers.

Far from being a definitive object, every track is now a reservoir of source material in the same way that *Kid A/Amnesiac*'s musical "deck" of cards is. In a strange way, it's a return to the very dawn of recorded music publishing with its printed song sheets and multiple cardboard "covers" (hence the name) advertising the different artists who had made their own recorded interpretations of a given song.

As Radiohead gear up in the wake of *Amnesiac* to release more and more of their music via the internet, they may find their long standing desire to control every aspect of its content and dissemination quickly becoming unworkable. It will be interesting to see how they come to terms with this new dynamic.

08 DOLLARS AND CENTS

A moody slice of political reverie, "Dollars and Cents" is a heartfelt tale of No Logo Lilliputians rising up against the globalist Gulliver: "We are the dollars and cents/And the pounds and pence, and yeah/We're going to crack your little souls/Crack your little souls".

This is something that Thom had personal experience of when, in the company of Bono and other like-minded Jubilee 2000 protesters, he came butt up against The System in June 1999 with an attempt to deliver Jubilee 2000's "Drop The Debt" petition (asking governments to write off Third World debt) to the G8's summit in Cologne. Not only were the protesters denied the hoped-for photo-opportunity of handing the petition into the front of the conference building, they were, as Thom ruefully told *The Wire*, "made to walk down the back streets, and it was fucking surreal – we had these German military police escorting us down a tiny pedestrian shopping street, we're carrying this fucking banner, surrounded by bemused shoppers."

"The point is that the most important political issues of the day have been taken out of the political arena," he continued. "They're being discussed by lobby groups paid for, or composed of, ex-members of corporations. And they spend a lot of effort trying to exclude the public because it's so inconvenient."

The form in which we have the track is, actually, the result of editing down an eleven minute improvisation, a technique which is once again reminiscent of early 70s band Can. "It's that Holger thing of chop-chop-chop," Thom

has recalled, "making what seems like drivel into something coherent."

In a sense that harks back to *Pablo Honey*, the last four songs on *Amnesiac* are where the not-unrelated process of thematic "reshuffling" starts to become just that bit too audible simply by reason of familiarity. Compelling though "Dollars and Cents" is in isolation, in context its musical skeleton pokes a little too visibly through the surface magic, breaking the spell.

Its atmosphere and jazzy rhythmic groove is very similar to "Knives Out", for example, from which it's separated by only one track. The rolling harmonic basis of the song, which forms the platform for Indian/overtonal meditation, is a technique already very familiar from both versions of "Morning Bell". The lovely string swoops and orchestral haze are "Pyramid Song" as if transported to Bollywood. Thom's lyrics, melody and delivery have the district air of *Kid A*'s "Optimistic" writ large.

It's interesting to speculate in what context the track might have been heard if *Kid A* and *Amnesiac* had been released as one double album, although even there, of course, the constraints of programming a single CD still have a bearing. Perhaps the brave new world of downloads, multi-gigabyte hard drives and endlessly flexible play lists really does hold the answer.

09 HUNTING BEARS

While by no means epic in scale, this short (2'01") instrumental duet between Thom's roving guitar and a complementing keyboard has an important function on the album. It's a contemplative backward glance before the final push to the finish.

The gently distorted but bright 60's Doors/Captain Beefheart guitar sound, Indian feel (i.e. the way that it smokily crawls up and around the overtones) and harmonic fixation of the piece neatly compresses several of the album's musical "themes". It evokes, for example, the introduction to "I Might Be Wrong", fusing keyboard and guitar in one, as much as it does "Pyramid Song". This fusion is echoed in the very "organic" playing style of the keyboard, which is set to play the most basically digital sine wave. Around it, all the swathes of noise sublimate, everything still further. It's quite the timbrel tone poem.

Its title is most probably a reference to the manically gleeful, vaguely political and seemingly hostile cartoon bears found throughout in the artwork of both *Kid A* and *Amnesiac*.

10 LIKE SPINNING PLATES

This track has perhaps the most unusual origin of any the band have ever recorded, being partly made up of an earlier song called "I Will" played backwards. "We'd turned the tape around," Thom told *The Wire*, "and I was in another room, heard the vocal melody coming backwards and thought, 'That's miles better than the right way round'. Then we spent the rest of the night trying to learn the melody."

He didn't stop there either, and grafted the reverse phonetics onto some wholly new, forward-going words so well that if you didn't know otherwise you would think the first verse was simply running backwards as part of the original track. The lyrics have yet to be published, but the heroic folk at followmearound.com have made out the following: "While you make pretty speeches/I'm being cut to shreds/You feed me to the lions/A delicate balance".

The first line is so "distorted" that it's very difficult to hear the words, but the rest seem to be accurate. Thom Yorke is one singer who obviously doesn't need technology to "process" his vocals, and the performance is quite a tribute to the acuity of his musical ear and vocal technique.

In the second verse, we get the comparisons to this process feeling "like spinning plates" and also like living in cloud-cuckoo-land. The metaphor of the title is a very evocative one, and obviously relates well to the tracks reversed hi-hat and synth sounds too. As to the original inspiration for the lyrics, some of Thom's post *Kid-A* thoughts on the music business promotional "machine" may offer a clue: "You have to remember that coming back into the lions' den was not easy, especially for me personally. It meant bringing back ghosts that made me shut down in the first place, so a lot of the decisions we made, and what we chose to do, was to avoid the normal giant cogs turning and crushing." It is thus similar subject matter to *The Bends*, perhaps, but expressed in a strikingly different way.

In interviews, Thom frequently mentions Kraftwerk in relation to this song but psycho-acoustics being what they are, it's not really apparent why until you reverse the track. At this point, the influence of the German band's analogue pulses and circling harmonies becomes very apparent. As it stands, the latter covers very similar ground to "Pyramid Song" but appropriately enough does so in reverse. Above these meditative remnants of the formerly rather driving "I Will" (now not dissimilar in effect to the opening guitar atmospheres of "Lucky") the band contribute additional "scintillations" in a manner not dissimilar to "Treefingers".

"In terms of trying to get somewhere new," Thom said to *Mojo*. "I think 'Spinning Plates' is the best on the whole record for me. When I listen to it in the car, it makes the doors shake."

"I ... heard the vocal melody coming backwards and thought, 'That's miles better than the right way round' "

11 LIFE IN A GLASSHOUSE

As the title suggests, "Life In A Glasshouse", is another tale of Radiohead's experience of life in the public eye. However, it operates from an intensely different angle than the previous track or indeed *The Bends*. As venerable as the song sounds, dating back to *OK Computer* days and briefly featuring in *Meeting People Is Easy*, it concerns the strange way that fame can both provide a privileged platform from which to speak, and at the same time be used to undermine the credibility of whatever might be said from it. It's a doleful New Orleans funereal for free speech in the "communication" age.

"I'm desperate for people to understand the words [to "Life In A Glasshouse"] because they're really important," Thom told *Mojo*. "It began after I read this interview with the wife of a very famous actor who the tabloids completely hounded for three months like dogs from hell. She got copies of all the papers with her photo in them and she pasted them up all over the house, over all the windows, so that all the cameras that were outside on her lawn only had their own images to photograph. I thought that was brilliant. From there, it developed into a complete rant about tabloid journalism destroying people at will, tying people to the stake and watching them burn – an activity that seems to be particularly rife in this country [Great Britain]."

Radiohead have themselves had acute experience of such media intrusion. Their public honesty regarding their political opinions has been met in some quarters with sneering accusations of hypocrisy, and the band has been "charged" with railing against the greed of multi-national corporations whilst simultaneously collaborating with them in the creation of million-dollar fortunes for all concerned. It's a tricky point, and the contradiction is one the band are not unaware of.

"We're screaming hypocrites. No, we are!" Thom self-deprecatingly exclaimed to *The Wire*. "Because we are right at the sharp end of the sexy, sassy MTV eye-candy lifestyle thing that they're trying to sell to the rest of the world. Unfortunately, if you're interested in actually being heard, you have to work within the system."

The funereal tone of "Life In A Glasshouse" would seem to suggest that despite the brave face, it's a situation the band find deeply troubling and as they increasingly strive to engage their public more directly via the internet, it's hard not to see these efforts as an attempt to challenge the status quo. Despite their fame and any contradictions arising from it, Radiohead would not unreasonably feel they should have the same right to express their thoughts on the world as anyone else. It's clearly their anger that certain factions of the media attempt to proscribe such basic freedoms that fuels this song.

"Rupert Murdoch has achieved this mind control trick" Thom has mused, "by getting his papers to work in a spectrum where it's very easy to dismiss any art that skirts towards Planet Politics.

"Because clearly he feels that's not where artists should be. So his papers instantly negate anything you do, and make you look ridiculous when you try to go anywhere beyond Geri Halliwell-land."

The lyrics support this point: "Once again packed like frozen food and battery hens/Think of all the starving millions/Don't talk politics and don't throw stones/Your royal highnesses". The overall message of the song is "I'm a reasonable man" so "get off my case", which is, of course, exactly where *Amnesiac* came in.

The album version of "Life In A Glasshouse" is a little like a reversed version of "Motion Picture Soundtrack". It begins with incandescent computer " cut-ups", perhaps recalling the fate of all that tabloid newsprint, before shuffling into distinctly less hi-tech territory. It's interesting to note that shorn of this album context, the cuts are cut from the full-length version of the song included on the "Knives Out" single.

The sense of mournful nostalgia is expertly conjured up by Thom's dog-tired vocal and the plaintive, tragic-comic caterwauling of a Mardi Gras band led by British "trad" jazz legend Humphrey Lyttelton. In suitably death-defying spirit, "Humph" played the session only one day after being released from hospital following open-heart surgery.

After two albums from the same session, there are as many musical references to previous tracks as you might expect. "Life In A Glasshouse" recalls the "down on my luck" scuzziness of "Motion Picture Soundtrack", the funereal country blues major/minor obsessiveness of "Morning Bell", the early jazz chord sequences of "You And Whose Army?", the instrumental multiplicity of "The National Anthem" and even the pentecostal origins of "Pyramid Song". As an album closer, the track is not as traditionally effective as some of its memorable predecessors, but perhaps that lingering sense of anti-climax is precisely the point.

Even with the "wobbles" noted during the composition process, and a slight overall sense of ambiguity regarding its relationship between variety and cohesion, *Amnesiac* is a very strong album indeed. Were it produced by any other band than Radiohead, with the myriad critical issues and baggage that inevitably surround them, it would most likely be regarded as a masterpiece: and, on aesthetic and creative grounds, many fair-minded listeners would accept no lesser a verdict.

I MIGHT BE WRONG:
live recordings

The euphoria that greeted the release of the "more accessible" *Amnesiac* was raised to an even higher pitch by the excitement surrounding the continuation of Radiohead's "tent" tour.

In the US, the band's progress made the quantum leap from music magazines to daily newspapers with an irresistible combination of innovative "anti-establishment" internet-enabled methodology, blue chip-critical acclaim for the musically hard-to-fathom "most important band in the word" and, last but certainly not least, gigantic commercial success. As Radiohead's status was upgraded from "successful cult group" to "must-see cultural event", the country succumbed in a way that drew many comparisons to The Beatles' invasion almost forty years earlier.

While it might have been commercially inevitable in the circumstances that a live recording of some description would be issued in the tour's wake, what was unusual was its scale and quality. Variously recorded at concerts on the European leg of the tour, including hometown Oxford, *I Might Be Wrong: Live Recordings* showcases a band at the height of its powers.

Radiohead's remarkably consistent musical focus, allowing them to "write" on stage as effectively as they "play" in the studio, means that their studio and live work has far greater unity of purpose than most bands. Each is a stage in the others' overall development, and both a part of a greater continuum. That said, the two contexts are obviously very different, and it's remarkable how, within one overall musical space, the extra energy and change of

focus that live performance entails can spin things around so dramatically. So it is with *I Might Be Wrong* from the very outset.

THE NATIONAL ANTHEM

In its original form on *Kid A*, "The National Anthem" is a measured, contemplative piece, far from the kind of track needed to convincingly open a record. Here, the song is transformed. Shorn of its swirling jazz and orchestral elements, it becomes a tightly ticking album-opening machine gliding inexorably forwards on the metallic runners of Colin's bass.

Under the gently circling searchlight beams of Jonny's onde martenot, Thom ties to squeeze this all new-found energy into the space where the melody's former dreaminess still lives. Working a double shift as crooning banshee and human beat-box, his churning "vocal percussion" is a revelation.

I MIGHT BE WRONG

Once againthe studio niceties (this time those of *Amnesiac*) are done away with, as Radiohead get their heads down for swamp boogie à la Studio 54. The guitar groove is far nastier and more acute than the album version, Colin is evidently having great fun with his Bernard Edwards licks, and it's always nice to hear tambourine on a Radiohead record, if only for the novelty. If Nile Rodgers had taken guitar lessons form Captain Beefheart, this is what Chic might have sounded like. The rather nice " jug band" synth from the original is quite sorely

```
LES ARENES
FREJUS

RADIOHEAD
17-06/00 19:30

CADO
CONDIN
DEC 28060045
        15@659
20-04/00 19 15

AUCHAN    TN
PRIX 180 DOP
LOCATION 17 ABP

AUCHAN MARSEILLE
CABINE
536693
```

```
LES ARENES 83600 FREJUS
Rue Henri Vadon
TRAFIC RESTREINT ET ADAM PRESENTENT
RADIOHEAD
+ SUPPORT
SAMEDI 17 JUIN 2000 19h30
PLACEMENT LIBRE
(PLACES ASSISES NON GARANTIES)
Prix : 180.00 Frs + 17.00 Frs frais de location
536693    AUCHAN    TN
```

missed, though, as it provided an important extra dimension to things. Without its rhythmic "cushioning", Thom's vocal sounds a little unsure of where to put itself.

MORNING BELL

This is *Kid A*'s 5/8 blues lament reading of the song as compared to *Amnesiac*'s horror-show. It's a far more swung version, however. With the electric piano set so starkly against Thom's tremulously tortured vocal, the whole song starts to mutate strangely into Supertramp *Crime Of The Century* territory. Presumably as an attempt to rectify this situation, Phil Selway's "trucking" hi-hats are given an extra push in the mix.

Overall it's a pretty much what you would expect from a live rendition of the song, although one still wonders how Jonny manages on cue to get his guitar to sound like electric power lines scrubbed with a sander. The polyrhythmic "two against three across bars of five" guitar scratches towards the end of the song are also a nice touch. Ed's Elvis Presley-like backing vocals are too cool to need comment upon.

LIKE SPINNING PLATES

The rolling, Michael Nyman-esque piano accompaniment to this version of the song is as charming as it is completely unexpected. After the reverse studio trickery of *Amnesiac*, what to do with the song live must have been quite a puzzle. This isn't only a far more satisfying solution than just loading up the sampler and replaying the original; it actually adds a whole new dimension to the song. The piano figurations have more similarity to the original's pulsing Kraftwerk inspired blips and blobs than you might imagine: you just have to find a way of playing *Amnesiac* backwards to find out!

In this simplified arrangement, the track's plaintive qualities can come through in a way slightly masked on the original. Thom leaves the phonetic trickery at the studio door and concentrates instead on emoting, which he does to wonderful effect. Delicate and intensely personal, this track is one of the of the album's absolute highpoints – a real showstopper.

IDIOTEQUE

Although "Idioteque" is perhaps the most electronic track on *Kid A*, this live version finds the laptop swiftly cast aside. The first part of the song is essentially just voice, digital keyboard and drums, with a few cling-clanging beeps added, but still it is absolutely compelling.

The mechanical elements and percussion first provide a pokey, rigid framework which Thom's breathlessly stressed vocal can then collapse over like melting wax. When the drums crash in for the second verse, however, he locks into them like a dervish. His rhythmic sense is fantastic, echoing the vocal percussion of "The National Anthem", and the way the energised crowd can be heard singing along in the background is also engaging. Together with the band's after song on-stage noises, the audience have a really important part to play in enhancing the contrast between human and machine. The song's climax sees the humans well and truly triumphant, as ever more crashing drums and Thom's rap bury the world's first heavy-metal Gameboy solo.

EVERYTHING IN ITS RIGHT PLACE

Although "transformation" is an important part of *Kid A*'s studio version of "Everything In Its Right Place", not many fans would foresee how this track would translate to the stage. The rarefied, if still groovy, computer assisted meditation of the studio is here transformed into what's best described as a soulful, psychedelic Stax. It just goes to show that there really is nothing new under the sun.

After a bit of "tuning up" (getting everything in its right place) reminiscent of live Queen, a really groovy bass part from Colin underpins Thom's

echoing vocal and the impressively mewing Ray Charles-like electric piano. Colin cites Stax/Booker T bassist Donald "Duck" Dunn (as also featured in *The Blues Brothers*) as a major influence, and there's an intensity about the relentlessly enfolding chromatic piano and bass that's very reminiscent of the classic "Green Onions".

Although the longest song on the album, at over seven minutes, "Everything In The Right Place" nevertheless has very spare instrumental resources: just vocals, electric piano, bass and light drums/percussion. The extra space is, of course, left for the "orchestra" of electronic noise that slowly builds up as the rest of the band, and Jim Warren's sound crew, sample and transform what's gone before.

DOLLARS AND CENTS

The looser, more dub-heavy atmosphere of this live version of the track actually works far better than the version on *Amnesiac*, providing a more logical connection between the propulsive ska-influenced bass and percussion and the atmospherics above. The energetically slicing guitars in particular seem a lot happier in this new context, and Thom's vocal has a far greater dramatic range and depth.

As previously mentioned, these kind of two-chord "atmosphere" songs ("Stop Whispering" at the very dawn of the band's career being a prime example) are notoriously difficult to translate into studio terms as what the song is really about are all the things that work best on stage; groove, interaction, atmosphere and dramatic inspiration. "The more concerts we do," Jonny told *The Wire*, "the more dissatisfied we get with trying to reproduce the live sound on the record. In a way it can't be done and that's a relief, really. When you just accept that, recording becomes a different thing."

TRUE LOVE WAITS

Although new on record, this is actually quite an old song, first debuted live in duet form at the band's December 1995 show at the Luna Theatre, Brussels. Here, in solo Thom plus acoustic guitar form, it tells a desperate tale of self-abasement and denial, a dark flip-side to the Hollywood myth that true love waits: "I'll drown my beliefs/To have you be in peace/I'll dress like your niece/To wash your swollen feet/Just don't leave, don't leave". If this is what it takes to keep the beloved, one ponders, maybe it's time for a change of girlfriend.

It's obviously hard for any song, or work of art, to do justice to the depths of a very close relationship, something the title of the original track "I Might Be Wrong" seems to imply. Given the unique closeness, understanding and even interdependence that exists between the Radiohead and their audience, it's difficult to think of a better way of closing this most intimate of encounters.

I Might Be Wrong:Live Recordings was released in the UK on November 12, 2001 and in the US on the following day, and reached numbers 23 and 44 respectively in the charts. Although automatically, by reason of its length, considered an album for chart purposes, band and record company tend to regard it as more of an extended EP, and there's still at least one more album to come as part of the Radiohead's original record deal with Capitol/EMI. There is no doubt that, after the amazing musical journey Radiohead have made in the course of eighteen years and, in the last near-decade, five (and a half!) remarkable albums, several million people round the world, will be looking forward to it intensely.

B-SIDES AND REMIXES

I Might Be Wrong may soon become a suitable subtitle to any one version of Radiohead tracks, as technology catches up with their ever ongoing musical development. The way that the band's songs have evolved through multiple versions in the laboratory of live performance seems increasingly likely to be mirrored (as in the case of *Kid A/Amnesiac*'s "Morning Bell") by multiple versions, live recordings (official and otherwise) and webcasts, all available immediately over broadband internet to your computer desktop.

In the good old pre-download days, if you wanted to follow a band's development between albums you did it via their singles and B-sides. In Radiohead's case these are legion, and almost as many additional songs have been released as B-sides as there are tracks on their first four albums.

Whilst Radiohead's five albums to date are undeniably the home of their best contemporary material, there are certainly occasional gems to be unearthed in this vast pile of work "in progress". The incredible complexity of the way that these extra tracks were released in various countries round the world precludes any hope of a chronological assessment, and an alphabetical overview is by far the best option.

A REMINDER

This is one of the band's very best B-sides. Thom recalled to the web site followmearound.com that, "'A Reminder' was written in one of those days off you have on a tour, where all you can do is sit in your hotel room because there"s nothing to do. I had got no idea where we were and there was just nothing to do at all. And I had this idea of someone writing a song, sending it to someone, and saying, 'If I ever lose it, you just pick up the phone and play me this song back to remind me'."

The lyric is very touching, after its initial bluster, and blessed with beautiful music (appropriately similar in atmosphere to "The Tourist") and a great performance. The track doesn't really put a foot wrong. Adding to the sense of travel and dislocation (unless, that is, you happen to be from the Czech Republic) is the opening ambience, complete with platform announcements from a Prague metro station

The track was first released in the UK with "Paranoid Android" (CD2) and later in the US as part of "Airbag"/"How Am I Driving?"

BANANA CO

Apart from the fact that "Oh, Banana Co" inwardly rhymes so well, the motivation for this folky but (in the chorus particularly) Beatles-esque song is Radiohead"s well-founded mistrust of multinationals, which they later writ large in tracks like *Amnesiac*'s "Optimistic".

The original, and rather charming, acoustic/twelve-string guitar version of the song, released with 1993's "Pop Is Dead", was ecorded as part of a session for Cheshire's Signal Radio. Later re-recorded by the whole band for a special benefit compilation (Axe The Act) opposing 1994's unpopular UK Criminal Justice Bill, the new, far more driving version found a home on CD2 (blue) of the 1996 "Street Spirit" single.

BISHOP"S ROBES

This song, recorded in the same three-day period as "Lucky" and "Talk Show Host" and like the latter released with "Street Spirit", is an impassioned condemnation of Thom's "bastard" ex-headmaster at Abingdon, one Michael St. John Parker Esq., hence the academic "bishop's" robes of the title. "He was a power-crazy, lunatic, evil, petty little man with ridiculous sideburns who used to flick his hair across his head to hide his bald patch," a vengeful Thom told Mick St. Michael. "I really grew up with a hatred for [him] because he was one fucked-up guy."

As all five Radiohead members were ex-pupils of Mr Parker, it goes without saying that this atmospheric song is performed with some feeling. Musically quite similar to "Lucky", there's also a chord change or two from Roberta Flack's "Killing Me Softly", which is certainly appropriate, if possibly unintentional.

The tension between rock music and education is as old as the invention of the teenager, and apart from any of his other sins, Mr Parker earned Thom's lasting enmity when he banned the nascent Radiohead from rehearsing on the school premises. "It was when he banned music that I really knew I hated him," Thom recalled. "I still hate him, and if I see or hear of him I get this deep sinking feeling." Confirmation, once again, that Abingdon days were very far from being the happiest of Thom's life.

CLIMBING UP THE WALLS

The UK release of "Karma Police" in

1997 included two remixes (on CD2) of this most terrifying of tracks from *OK Computer*. Although a tasty and very well-executed piece of chill out, the Zero 7 mix somehow lacks enough sense of the song's original meaning. As the song winds down, things do get a bit more imaginative with a twisted Latin take on things coming into play, but by then one can"t help thinking it's a little late in the day. The Fila Brazilia mix takes things in a more lo-fi dub direction, but is rather perfunctory. There's really no sense of a meaningful engagement with the original.

COKE BABIES

Although dating from the same February 1993 release as "Faithless The Wonder Boy", (both tracks backed "Anyone Can Play Guitar"), this ruminative, shoegazing special is far more forward-looking, and prefigures later more atmospheric Bends era work such as "Bullet Proof". Lyrically, the song may be an early if extremely vague assault on the coke-taking little piggies of "Paranoid Android" but it's difficult to be entirely certain; of 37 words in the song, 14 are "easy"!

CUTTOOTH

In the same way that the Mingus-inspired moodiness of "Pyramid Song" was echoed in its B-sides, the more upbeat "Knives Out" spawned its own crop of associated tracks. The first track on "Knives Out" CD1, "Cuttooth" is the most straightforwardly Beatles-influenced track the band have released since "Karma Police" and feels as though it wouldn't be that out of place dropped into the middle of the "White" album.
The lyrics are a meditation on the potentially destructive, stymieing effects of "a little bit of knowledge" and the possible ways to circumvent them: "I don't know why I feel so tongue-tied/I don't know why I feel so skinned alive/I'll find another skin to wear". This, this author feels, is something that all survivors of higher education can sympathise with.

FAITHLESS, THE WONDER BOY

Despite the chorus of this 1993 back-up to "Anyone Can Play Guitar" being formed by incessant repetitions of "[I] can't put the needle in", the subject of the song is not drug-taking but rather getting, or more pertinently not getting, revenge on a host of tormentors (friends, Mum and Dad etc.): "I want the toys of other boys/I want a knife and a gun and things/But Mum and Dad will not give in". In terms of both verse structure and subject matter (that old chestnut domestic frustration) it has considerable parallels with "Prove Yourself".

FAST TRACK

The "instrumental" "Fast Track" (the second track on "Pyramid Song" CD2) has a similar mutant feel to "The Amazing Sounds Of Orgy" but is slightly more upbeat. With choice samples from *Amnesiac* and beyond "scatting" over a skippy jazzy beat, the piece feels like the aural equivalent of a Ren & Stimpy cartoon. This is the sonic world of the 1950s and 1960s twisted by time, technology and modern sensibility.

FOG

Originally premiered live as "Alligators In New York Sewers", "Fog", the last track on "Knives Out" CD2, is what happens when a wholesome upbeat song gets molested by menacing horror film atmospherics. Musically, the classic pop tune surrounded by billowing soundscapes evokes an ambient Phil Spector, or a Brian Eno-produced early-period Beatles.
Lyrically, however, it"s a different, far less benign story. A little child runs,

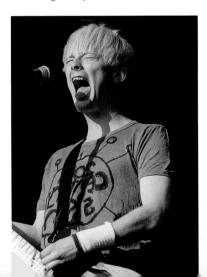

trapped forever in a house, while glowing fog rises up from the sewers. Meanwhile, far beneath the streets, baby alligators are growing. As might be expected, all of the above is psychological metaphor: "Anything you want it can be done,/How did you go bad?/Did you go bad?/Some things will never wash away." By no coincidence, one imagines, this totally contradicts the message of "Worrywort", the previous song on the single: a neat bit of programming.

HOW CAN YOU BE SURE?

This lilting Pablo Honey-era ballad, which again revisits the complex world of intimate emotional relationships, is a pretty straightforward retread of territory staked out in previous decades by Dylan and Bruce Springsteen, and then subsequently claimed by U2 on The Joshua Tree. It's vaguely notable for being the first and only time that the band have used an additional backing singer, Dianne Swann. Eventually partnering "Fake Plastic Tress" in the UK and US it was initially entitled "When I'm Like This" when released in Japan.

HOW I MADE MY MILLIONS

Although there are several first takes in the Radiohead canon, this is perhaps the only raw demo that's made it to final release.
Having just written this slice of melancholic introspection at home on his rather ancient sounding piano, Thom recorded it straight into his MiniDisc recorder. And what are the ambient sounds in the background? Thom's girlfriend, Rachel, doing the housework! The lyrics are somewhat diffuse, but reading between the lines the song is another of Thom's takes on relationship torment. It's a very strong, if obviously improvisatory, performance and, given the lyrics, one that the unusual recording setting seems to enhance, which is most likely why the band decided the "demo" was already its own final product.

The song's UK release was in January 1998, on "Karma Police" CD1, where it followed "Palo Alto": a very effective juxtaposition.

INDIA RUBBER

In essence "India Rubber" is a swooning 1960s ballad in the Scott Walker/Burt Bacharach tradition, which the band have fun updating with then (c.1995) modern production techniques and atmospheres. Released with "Fake Plastic Trees" the track's chief interest is in the way the band use it as a sketch pad for ideas and arrangements (sampled vocals, loops and lyrical melodies put against remorseless techno drums in the midst of shimmering atmospherics) which would find proper expression on *Kid A* and *Amnesiac*. The title and lyrics refer to a severe case of the infatuation "wobbles".

INSIDE MY HEAD

At one time mooted as a possible second single for the band (the eventual A-side was, thankfully, "Creep"), this energetic Pixies-influenced rocker was one of the first songs the band wrote just after signing with EMI/Parlophone and its subject is, consequently, fears of big business and "contamination": "What do you want from me now you got me/Now my fingers bleed now they stare at me".

Equivocation (or at least the pretence of same) about things that you broke your back to accomplish in the first place is rather approved of in the UK, where it comes under the heading of "gentlemanly conduct" and "polite self-depreciation". As Thom all too correctly diagnoses: "I've got a disease, an English disease". A live version of the track, with a great guitar and voice "solo", was substituted for the original studio version on "Creep's later UK reissue.

KILLER CARS

This is the second of Thom's songs dealing with his long-standing dislike of the eponymous vehicles (the others are "Stupid Car" and *OK Computer*'s "Airbag"). The lyrics are a lexicon of anxiety, and it's not hard to see where the later inspiration for "Airbag" came from: "Too hard on the brakes again/What if these brakes just give in?/What if they don't get out of the way?" So vexed is Thom by the vehicles that the track has been released in no less than three different forms.

The first is a live acoustic version from the band's 1993 show at the Chicago Metro, and appears on the 12" UK reissue of "Creep". You can tell just how freaked out Thom genuinely is by the heartfelt nature of the performance. The second version, appearing on February 1995's "High And Dry"/"Planet Telex" (blue) CD2 is a much more conventional rock workout that seems to combine influences of early Queen and uncharacteristically Bowie (Ziggy Stardust meets the distinctive minor cadences of "You're My Best Friend"). Bringing up the rear is the Mogadon-like version released six months later on "Just's (red) CD1. Slower and mellower than the previous version, this also features perhaps the only "police radio" solo in existence.

KINETIC

The last track on "Pyramid Song" CD2, "Kinetic" certainly lives up to its billing and

The musically kinetic Charles Mingus

is a very plastic, dub-inclined take on the "jazz cartoon" ambience of its "Pyramid Song" fellows ("The Amazing Sound Of Orgy" and "Fast Track"). The lyrics are an exhortation to "please keep moving", and that's exactly what the track does, recycling all manner of sounds, treatments and styles heard elsewhere within its abstract, but basically jazzy, framework. It sounds like Charles Mingus let loose on modern technology, and the closing "Buddy Rich in space" drum solo is particularly neat.

LEWIS (MISTREATED)

This is a fascinating little piece which anticipates the multi-sectional feel of tracks on *The Bends* and thereafter. The mood changes radically every few bars, flipping from the Velvet Underground to the Small Faces/Kinks/Britpop, to Hendrix and back again. The lyrics are "friendly" words of advice to "a low corporate" drone deemed unlikely to ever amount to anything: "Lewis, save yourself the pain/You'll never get there". Whether the mistreated Lewis is based on Oxford-based fictional detective Inspector Morse's similarly named hapless sidekick is sadly not known.

LOZENGE OF LOVE

The title of this folky but at the same time quite Beatles-esque Bends-era piece (there are shades of "Within You, Without

You" in the evolution of the vocal melody and its vocal/guitar setting) was taken from a Philip Larkin poem entitled "Sad Steps". Lyrically exploring the dysfunctional aspects of some relationships, Thom's vocal is terrific, and an early display of the spellbinding emoting that listeners would soon take for granted. Overall the song is rather lovely, and perhaps anticipates the Indian atmospherics of *Amnesiac*.

LULL

This is a short but pretty song that extracts the nursery elements (chiming guitar and glockenspiel) of *OK Computer*'s "No Surprises" and moulds them into a trancey but intense groove appropriate to the title. The lyric reveals that said "Lull" is the calm after a nasty emotional storm, and the latter is still discernible in the song's circling guitar arpeggios, restive feel, and closing guitar scrape seemingly borrowed from "Climbing Up The Walls" It was released in the UK with "Karma Police" (CD1) in August 1997.

MAQUILADORA

Originally called "Interstate Five" and drawn from the band's experiences while on the post "Creep" tour of North America, this is an early manifestation of Radiohead's social conscience. The lyrics of the song raise the question of who actually pays to sustain the lifestyle of the American Dream, accompanied by some candid thoughts about the group's own place in the scheme of things: "Fast Toyota, burns rubber/Useless rockers from England/Good times had by all/Just swallow your guilt and your conscience." Given that "maquiladora" is Spanish slang for the fences that US-owned corporations use to surround their Mexican factories, the answer to the question posed would seem to be "the rest of the world".

The song, released on the "High And Dry" single, makes effective use of dynamic and musical contrasts to illustrate the changing spin of the lyrics, and might

be best summarised as *The Bends* heading south of the border. As expected in this kind of wide ranging rocker there's a number of musical influences floating about, and in addition to the unlikely pairing of Los Lobos and the guitar work of Queen's Brian May, there's a hint of Marc Bolan thrown in too. Relishing the dramatic possibilities of the song, and the opportunity to give the establishment a good kicking, Thom delivers one of his very best punk-tinged vocals.

MEETING IN THE AISLE

An early taste of the sonic world of Kid A/Amnesiac, this instrumental piece is a prototype of the later "Dollars And Cents" and features almost identical sliding guitars and Indian-influenced string lines. Released with the "Karma Police" single (CD1) in May 1997, and later as part of "Airbag/How Am I Driving?", the band also aptly used it as an entrance song for their 1998 concert tour.

MELATONIN

Released in the UK on "Paranoid Android", this track also formed part of the US-only OK Computer B-side round-up "Airbag"/ "How Am I Driving?"

The song's title relates to the sleep-regulating hormone that, although banned in the UK, has become popularised as a home-administered "miracle" anti-aging cure in the US. The lyric has an air of ironic condemnation about this kind of "off the peg" usage and continues the EP's vein of social critique. Following on from the complex "Polyethylene", this song has a metrical quirk all of its own, and its music is grouped into repeating patterns of 3 and 5 beat bars, working well against the diaphanous synth strings. Overall, it has a distinct flavour of Kraftwerk about it, and so anticipates aspects of *Kid A/Amnesiac*.

MILLION $ QUESTION

A spirited punk rock sandwich, this track, written at the same time and

covering similar post-record deal ground to "Inside My Head", is one of the band's best early B-sides. In this case, the song's lyrics focus on Thom's recent escape from hated part-time jobs, but there is a typical note of self-doubt tossed in at the end. The possibility of his making a mistake in leaving forms the quiz show question of the title.

MOLASSES

Recorded at *The Bends* Manor Studio sessions in June 1995, and released six months later with "Street Spirit", "Molasses" is another of the band's political numbers. Though tackling a very serious subject, the exploitation of Third World agriculture by multinational corporations alluded to in the earlier "Banana Co", it takes a similarly light approach, and is all the more effective for it. Featuring some outrageously tortured and in context rather funny rhymes: "I need someone else's glasses/Starving waitresses in plasters", it nevertheless gets its point across: "Shake hands, genocide, molasses". Musically the song is best and described as sweetly languid, having a 60's lounge feel about it. This use of "political" nostalgia would crop up again in the later, rather less light-hearted, "You and Whose Army?"

PALO ALTO

This is another slice of social commentary from the Noam Chomsky-quoting "Airbag"/"How Am I Driving" EP, which was previously released in the UK in January 1998 with "No Surprises" (CD1).

Positioned at the very heart of Silicon

Valley, Palo Alto is home to many of America's largest technology corporations including Xerox and Apple, truly the "city of the future" mentioned in the song's opening line. The lyric paints a terrifying Stepford Wives-like picture of a city inhabited by smiling, dehumanised people reduced to the level of automatons, no longer capable of normal human contact. It's not a cheerful vista, but it's certainly consistent with the overall theme of *OK Computer*.

"Palo Alto" is a great track, revisiting the band's early Pixies influences but putting them in the context of everything that Radiohead had heard since then. It's another of the band's very best B-sides.

PEARLY*
This track was one of the final fourteen short-listed for *OK Computer*; the other eventual casualty was "Polyethylene (Parts 1 & 2)". In the tradition of "Banana Co." and "Molasses", "Pearly*" is another political song dealing with Third World issues, but this time examining the way some of the latter"s citizens seek to "escape" their situation by pursuing the superficialities of the West: "Vanilla Milkshakes/From Hard Rock Cafes/That's where she got her sweet tooth/For white boys"

This is a terrifically atmospheric number, combining the 60s TV feel of "The Trickster" with the languid Latin feel of "Molasses" and a "Tomorrow Never Knows" drumbeat. The bouncing, John Barry-esque cimbalom solo (actually a guitar) is particularly evocative of Harry Palmer-type double-dealing. Released in the UK with "Paranoid Android", it also formed part of the US OK Computer B-side roundup "Airbag"/"How Am I Driving?"

PERMANENT DAYLIGHT
Originally part of the band's mid-1993 live set, this hypnotic piece was at one stage offered, unsuccessfully, for a slot on a soundtrack. Constantly varied but without distracting from the overall mood, "Permanent Daylight" does have the focussed air of a soundtrack experiment about it. Thom's vocal, directly derived

from the guitars, is a nice gloss if a tad perfunctory.

POLYETHYLENE (PARTS 1 & 2)
The lyrics of "Polyethylene", like those of "Pearly*", are a critique of superficiality but in an environment rather closer to home; that of the middle class lifestyle of "Maquiladora". Slightly abstract in nature, the lyric plays with the all-too-prevalent desire to enjoy the upside of a comfortable lifestyle without consequences: "Plastic bag middle class polyethylene/Decaffeinate/I'll let it/Unleaded/Keep all surfaces clean".

The music is interesting, as the song is a multi-sectional rocker like "The Bends" but with a twist. Whereas "Polyethylene Part 1" is a sparse Thom Yorke voice and guitar introduction in regular 4/4 time (four beats in a bar), "Part 2", in a manner similar to the way chemicals like polyethylene are actually made, "cracks" this intro into smaller units and then assembles them into complex "strings" of different length bars. This lends the song a shifting, unpredictable feel. The trouble is that the music itself isn't quite strong enough to warrant this level of attention, and overall the ambition of the song rather outstrips its resources.

Released in the UK with "Paranoid Android", the track also appeared on "Airbag/How Am I Driving?"

PLANET TELEX
This track has been released in a greater number of different versions than any other in the band's recorded repertoire .

Steve Osbourne"s "Hexadecimal" mix was released on the February 1995 CD1 (red) version of the "Planet Telex"/"High And Dry" single, and is a pretty dull slice of dub- influenced chill-out. The "LFO JD" mix

was released on the corresponding (blue) version (CD2) of the same single, and is very much better. LFO's Warp label origins show strongly, and in many ways the remix is a prototype for the electronica aspects of *Kid A* and *Amnesiac*. The triggered vocal loop early in the track, for example, is particularly reminiscent of "Everything In Its Right Place". Both remixes, as might be expected, formed part of the "Planet Telex"/"High And Dry" vinyl 12".

There was also a "Karma Sunra" version of the track released in August 1995 on the red (CD1) version of the "Planet Telex"/"High And Dry" single which also featured the "Mogadon" version of "Killer Cars". The DJ Shadow-led group U.N.K.L.E. produced this "illbient" mix, which works very well. The trace elements of the original are expanded by way of a Beatle-esque Indian vibe and in this context the "Strawberry Fields" flute line is rather witty. The final, spirited live version of the track is on the corresponding blue CD2 of the same track

POP IS DEAD
Although not strictly a B-side, "Pop Is Dead" was actually the band's final single of 1993. However, it deserves to be treated as a B-side for the simple reason that it's not very good. This, presumably, is why ithe track was left off *Pablo Honey* in the first place

Comedy, however ironic, only works when the underlying music is top class, and this fundamentally routine rocker tries to be a little too clever for its own good. A then contemporary commentary on the state of pop music, Thom described it as "a kind of epitaph of 1992", hence: "Pop is dead, long live pop/It died an ugly death by back catalogue".

PUNCHDRUNK LOVESICK SINGALONG
Released in September 1994 on "My Iron Lung's CD1 (blue), this song follows on from "The Trickster" in more ways than one, expanding the new "cinematic" feel still further whilst raising the soon to

Right: Pink Floyd, whose enveloping echoes made such an impression on Radiohead

Far right: Glastonbury 1994 – one of Radiohead's most important early gigs

be familiar ghost of Pink Floyd. In the verses particularly, the song is not only reminiscent of "Black Star" but also seems to anticipate *OK Computer*'s "The Tourist". "Punchdrunk" and "lovesick" are familiar Thom Yorke lyrical staples from "You" onwards, but the surprising major key chorus manages to put a fresh spin on things.

STUPID CAR
In its original form on 1992's "Drill" EP, this first song to deal with Thom's long-standing distrust of cars ("Killer Cars" and *OK Computer*'s "Airbag" would follow) is a rather doleful voice and guitar duet. Some of the lyrics are rather striking, though: "You got concrete eyes/And I cannot see your face" prefiguring the later metaphorical imagery of songs such as "Fake Plastic Eyes". A later re-recording, the Tinnitus Mix, appeared on 1993"s Volume 7 CD compilation.

TALK SHOW HOST
Recorded in the same three-day period as "Lucky" and "Bishop"s Robes", "Talk Show Host" joined *OK Computer*'s "Exit Music" in being featured in Baz Luhrman's remarkable film *Romeo and Juliet*. An additional mix by Massive Attack and Björk producer Nellee Hooper can be found on the film"s soundtrack album, and a further "Black Dog" mix of the track was also made.

In uncut form, the song was released with "Street Spirit" (on the blue CD1) and has more than a hint of Massive Attack about it. Its use of distorted drums, here of a suitably Billy Cobham-esqe nature, is a dry run for *OK Computer*'s "Airbag". As far as the lyrics go, they're remarkable for the lack of any direct connection with the subject of the title.

THE AMAZING SOUNDS OF ORGY
Amnesiac's "Pyramid Song", released in May 2001 was the band's first single since "No Surprises" over three years earlier. The second track on "Pyramid Song""s CD1, "The Amazing Sound Of Orgy", picks up

from the borrowed do-wop of "You And Whose Army?" to produce a dark slice of sci-fi mutant jazz – a Martian "Life In A Glasshouse".

The slappy, hollow percussion sounds that form such a prominent feature of the track are most probably long thin didgeridoo-like drums called "boo-bams" They certainly add to the mood-drenched *Twin Peaks* surrealism of the whole affair. The lyrics are as loaded with arresting images as they are incomprehensible, but buried in there somewhere, believe it or not, is a love song!

THE TRICKSTER
Released in September 1994 on the "My Iron Lung" CD1 (blue), this is a great song with a mutated 60s TV spy feel in the lyrics and verses contrasting with expansive metrically tricky choruses. It marks a real transition between the indie drive of Pablo Honey and the more expansive soundscapes of The Bends.

TRANSATLANTIC DRAWL
The final track on "Pyramid Song" CD1, "Transatlantic Drawl" kicks off as a punky workout the like of which those baffled by Kid A must have thought they'd heard the last of. After the first two verses, however, the needle suddenly skips to land in the "Palo Alto" chapel of rest. This kind of music is pretty disturbing even if straight, but "Transatlantic Drawl" not only twists things around harmonically, it also adds further saccharine weirdness by playing it on synthesised vocal sounds. If that's a picture of the afterlife, most people would choose to stay here.

The reason for this sudden musical shift might be found in the lyric. The existential angst that Thom feels in being "trapped in the society page" without knowing "what it means" is suddenly replaced by the urgent question: "Do you see light at the end of the tunnel?" Judging by the music of the second half, a near-death experience has provided him with the answers to both questions.

WORRYWORT
The second track on "Knives Out" CD2, this is another re-jigging of *Kid A/Amnesiac*'s musical elements, the Kraftwerk-inspired origins of "Like Spinning Plates" combined with the playful "hi-hat" cut-ups of the finished track, all set in the ambient soundscapes of "Treefingers". The way that filtered samples of Thom are overlaid with the hi-hats to make a 21st century version of "steam train" scat-jazz vocals is particularly cool.

Reprising similar territory to "I Might Be Wrong", "Worrywort" is a gentle meditation on the futility of worrying, and combines some homespun, down-to-earth sound advice with lovely poetic imagery: "There"s no use dwelling/On what might have been/Find yourself a moment/And go and get some wings"

YES I AM
A slow burning tirade against fickle, fair-weather friendship, "Yes I Am" was recorded at the same Jim Warren-chaired sessions that produced "Pop Is Dead" and "High And Dry". This song figured as part of the July 1993 UK re-release of "Creep".

"Yes I Am" seems to be an early prototype for later multi-sectional tracks such as "The Bends" and "Paranoid Android". Stylistically, it progresses from the laid back REM/U2 indie-dom of the opening to an outrageous "borrowing" of The Kink's "You Really Got Me" riff for the chorus. This is later superimposed with twisting chromatic guitar and sampled string lines.

YOU NEVER WASH UP AFTER YOURSELF
Recorded in one take at the band's "fruit farm" rehearsal come recording studio, this intimate miniature released on "My Iron Lung"s red CD2 focuses on the stultifying domestic minutiae of a stagnant life. This attention to lyrical detail and ability to paint such convincing small-scale dramas is a defining characteristic that separates the era of *The Bends* from that of the preceding *Pablo Honey*.

CHRONOLOGY

May 23, 1967
Phil Selway born in Hemingford Grey, Cambridgeshire.

April 15, 1968
Ed O"Brien born in Oxford.

October 7, 1968
Thom Yorke born in Wellingborough, Northamptonshire.

June 26, 1969
Colin Greenwood born in Oxford.

November 5, 1971
Jonny Greenwood born in Oxford.

1984
On A Friday form at Abingdon School, Oxfordshire.

1986 – 91
The band members disperse to various colleges and universities.

February 1987
On A Friday's first demo tape and press review.

Summer 1987

On A Friday's first live show at Jericho Tavern, Oxford.

October 1991
On A Friday record the "Manic Hedgehog" cassette at Chris Hufford and Bryce Edge's studio in Abingdon. Hufford and Edge are appointed as managers.

December 21, 1991
On A Friday sign a six-album deal with Parlophone.

March 1992

They change their name to Radiohead.

April 1992
Radiohead's first UK tour, supporting the Catherine Wheel

May 5, 1992
Radiohead release debut "Drill" EP.

September 21, 1992
"Creep" is released as single in UK but peaks at number 78.

October 21, 1992
Radiohead tour the UK, firstly with The Frank & Walters then with Kingmaker.

February 22, 1993
Debut album *Pablo Honey* released in UK.

April 20, 1993
Pablo Honey released in the US.

June 1, 1993
Radiohead tour US in support of *Pablo Honey*. "Creep" single peaks at number 34 in Billboard chart.

September 6, 1993
"Creep" is re-released in the UK and reaches number 7.

September 17, 1993
Radiohead begin a US tour supporting Belly.

May 1994
Radiohead tour Spain, Italy, Switzerland, Germany, UK, Japan, Hong Kong and Australia.

May 27, 1994
The band play the Astoria, London, and record the *Astoria London Live* video.

March 13, 1995
Radiohead release their second album, *The Bends*, in the UK. It peaks at number 6, then climbs back to number 4 the following year.

April 4, 1995
The Bends is released in the US.

May 26, 1995
Radiohead begin a short US tour in Boston, ending on June 15 in Los Angeles.

July 29-30, 1995
Radiohead play the National Bowl, Milton Keynes with REM, the Cranberries and Blur.

September 4, 1995
Radiohead record "Lucky" in five hours for War Child's *Help!* charity album.

September 8, 1995
Radiohead begin US tour supporting REM, then tour the States with Soul Asylum before headlining dates in Europe.

January 22, 1996
"Street Spirit" is released as a UK single and reaches number 5, Radiohead"s highest chart placing to date.

February 19, 1996
Thom Yorke and Brian Eno collect Freddie Mercury Award for their contributions to *Help!* at the UK's BRIT Awards.

April 4, 1996
The Bends goes gold in the US. UK platinum status soon follows.

June 1996
Radiohead begin recording *OK Computer* at Canned Applause and play the European festival circuit.

August 1996
They support Alanis Morissette across the US tour and contribute "Exit Music (For A Film)" to the soundtrack of *Romeo & Juliet*.

May 22, 1997
Radiohead preview material from *OK Computer* at a show in Barcelona, Spain.

June 8, 1997
The band play the first Tibetan Freedom Concert in New York.

June 16, 1997
OK Computer is released in the UK. It becomes Radiohead"s first number 1 album.

June 28, 1997
Radiohead headline the UK's Glastonbury Festival.

July 1, 1997
OK Computer is released in the US, reaching number 21.

August 29, 1997
Radiohead play "Karma Police" on *The Late Show with David Letterman*.

November 1997
The band sell out five nights at Wembley Arena, London.

December 1997
Radiohead are named Band Of The Year by *Rolling Stone* and *Spin. Q* and *NME* both declare *OK Computer* Album Of The Year.

February 26, 1998

Radiohead win a Grammy for Best

band's only European show of 1998, and proves to be their last gig for eighteen months.

January 1999
Radiohead re-convene in Paris to begin recording what will become the *Kid A* and *Amnesiac* albums.

March 1999
The recording sessions relocate first to Copenhagen, then to Batsford Park, Gloucestershire, and later to Radiohead's Oxfordshire studio.

June 13, 1999
Thom Yorke and Jonny Greenwood play a Tibetan Freedom Concert in Amsterdam.

December 1999

May 21, 2001
"Pyramid Song" becomes Radiohead's first UK single for three years. It reaches number 5 in the charts. They play European shows and festivals.

June 4, 2001
Radiohead release the *Amnesiac* album in the UK, with the US again following a day later. A product of the same sessions as *Kid A*, *Amnesiac* follows its twin to the top of the album charts in both countries (UK No. 1, US No. 2).

June 18, 2001
Radiohead begin a US tour in Woodlands, Texas.

July 7, 2001

DISCOGRAPHY

The way in which Radiohead's music has been disseminated around the world from its UK base, subject until recently to the demands of each separate territory and the ingenuity of its local marketing department, can only be described as labyrinthine. Such is the sophistication of the modern music and media business that a full discography covering every local repackaging, resequencing, formatting and promotion would not only fill a small book by itself, but also completely obscure the purpose of this one. The internet is, appropriately enough, now the only place were such data can sensibly be assembled and perused.

"You"
Recorded: October 1991

2. RADIOHEAD SINGLES, EPs AND MINI ALBUMS

"Drill"
CD/12"/cassette - limited
  edition of 3000
"Prove Yourself" (EP version)
"Stupid Car"
"You" (EP version)
"Thinking About You" (EP version).
UK: May 5, 1992 (101)

"Creep"
CD/12"/cassette – limited
  edition of 6000
"Creep"
"Lurgee"
"Inside My Head"

"Inside My Head" (live)
Limited-edition 12"
"Creep" (live acoustic version for
KROQ Radio LA)
"You" (live)
"Vegetable" (live)
"Killer Cars" (live)
Live tracks recorded at the
Chicago Metro, June 1993.
UK: September 6, 1993 (7)

"Stop Whispering" – US only
CD
"Stop Whispering" (Remix)
"Creep"
"Pop Is Dead"
"Inside My Head"
US: December 1993

"My Iron Lung"
CD(blue)/12"/cassette

"Fake Plastic Trees"
  CD(blue)/cassette
"Fake Plastic Trees"
"India Rubber"
"How Can You Be Sure?"
  CD(red)
"Fake Plastic Trees"
"Fake Plastic Trees" (acoustic)
"Bullet Proof... I Wish I Was"
  (acoustic)
"Street Spirit"
Acoustic tracks recorded at
  Eve"s Club, London.
  UK: May 15, 1995 (20)
  US version: July 11, 1995

"Just"
  CD(red)/cassette
"Just"
"Planet Telex" (Karma Sunra Mix)"
"Killer Cars" (Mogadon version)

" Maquiladora"
"How Can You Be Sure?"
"Just" (live)
US: February 27, 1996 (78)

"Paranoid Android"
CD1/7" (first two tracks only)
"Paranoid Android"
"Polyethylene (Parts 1&2)"
"Pearly*"
CD2
"Paranoid Android"
"A Reminder"
"Melatonin"
UK: May 26, 1997 (3)

"Karma Police"
CD1
"Karma Police"
"Meeting In The Aisle"
"Lull"

"Pyramid Song"
CD1/12"
"Pyramid Song"
"The Amazing Sounds Of Orgy"
"Trans-Atlantic Drawl"
CD2
"Pyramid Song"
"Fast Track"
"Kinetic"
UK: May 21, 2001 (5)

"Knives Out"
CD1/12"
"Knives Out"
"Cuttooth"
"Life In A Glasshouse" (full length version)
CD2
"Knives Out"
"Worrywort"
"Fog"

"Sulk"
"Street Spirit (Fade Out)"
UK: March 13, 1995 (4)
US: April 4, 1995 (88)

OK Computer
"Airbag"
"Paranoid Android"
"Subterranean Homesick Alien"
"Exit Music (For A Film)"
"Let Down"
"Karma Police"
"Fitter Happier"
"Electioneering"
"Climbing Up The Walls"
"No Surprises"
"Lucky"
"The Tourist"
  UK: June 16, 1997 (1)
  US: July 1, 1997 (21)

"Morning Bell"
"Like Spinning Plates"
"Idioteque"
"Everything In Its Right Place"
"Dollars And Cents"
"True Love Waits"
  UK: November 12, 2001 (23)
  US: November 13, 2001 (44)

4. VIDEO/DVD

The Astoria London Live Video
"You"
"Bones"
"Ripchord"
"Black Star"
"Creep"
"The Bends"
"My Iron Lung"
"Prove Yourself"

INDEX